THE FLOURISHING STUDENT

Every tutor's guide to promoting mental health, well-being and resilience in Higher Education

FABLE

First published in Great Britain by Practical Inspiration Publishing, 2017

© Fabienne Vailes, 2017

The moral rights of the author have been asserted

ISBN (print): 978-1-910056-59-2

ISBN (ebook): 978-1-910056-58-5 (Kindle)

ISBN (ebook): 978-1-910056-78-3 (ePub)

Practical Inspiration
PUBLISHING

Dedicated to my amazing and loving family and friends:

June, Bernard, Chantal, Louis, Lorraine and my wonderful husband and best friend Jason – without your support and help this book would never have happened.

And to my fabulous boys Thomas and Jack – I hope this Flourishing model serves and guides you throughout your childhood and beyond.

Acknowledgements

My heartfelt thanks to:

First of all, this book would not have happened without all the prior knowledge and skills I acquired with John Seymour (of JSnlp) who taught me all that I know about NLP and in particular all the NLP techniques I have used in this book and Adam Dacey (MindSpace) who introduced me to Mindfulness and showed me not only how to teach it but also how to introduce it into my daily life. I am forever indebted to you both!

Alison Jones, my publisher for believing in me and in this book. Thanks so much for providing me with the support and platform to transform the dreams into a reality.

Professor Corey Keyes and Dr Stanley Kutcher for allowing me to use their work and models as a base for my work and for spending some time discussing this over Skype.

Colleagues and experts (in particular, Mark Ames, Sarah Ashworth, Jeremy Christey, Ed Davis, Laurie Leitch, Amy Lewis, Knut Schroeder and Dominique Thompson) who shared their thoughts with me and agreed to give up some of their precious time to share their insights into this fascinating and important topic of mental health in HE and/or to connect me with other specialists.

Students and colleagues who allowed me to use their stories to write this book. You know who you are and I am very grateful to you all!

You have enabled and inspired me to create this flourishing student model.

All my colleagues and friends in the School of Modern Languages and outside university who spent some time reading this first draft and giving me feedback.

Foreword

What an exciting, helpful and much-needed new book this is. In 2016 the *Guardian* newspaper reported that the number of university students dropping out of university due to mental health problems has trebled in recent years. This was based on data published by the Higher Education Statistics Agency (HESA). Following this, there has been much debate in the media about 'mental health being the new university crisis'. I believe this book brings a much-needed balanced look at what is actually happening and how we can start to understand and address these issues using a practical and empirically sound approach.

Going to university is an important milestone in any person's life and students often have expectations that it will be an amazing experience, rich with learning, full of fun and excitement, studying subjects they are passionate about, and that they will leave university prepared to start well-paid job. Whilst this may be true for some students, for many university students the reality is struggling to cope with the workload, lots of exams and assessments, expectations and pressures from others to perform and gain good marks, financial worries, feeling lonely and juggling the constant demands on time for study, work and personal commitments.

When Fabienne first contacted me to be interviewed for her book, I was really intrigued by her idea and keen to be involved. For me, it fills a much-needed void in the literature around teaching and working in Higher Education. Fabienne and I had an interesting discussion around the issues she raises in the book and how the model that I use in my work, Professor Steve Peter's Chimp model, fits with these.

Whilst completing my PhD, I taught undergraduate modules and after completing my doctorate taught both undergraduate and masters level students. During this time, I was struck by how many of the students struggled to cope with the workloads and pressures of university life. What was concerning was that many universities struggled to identify this, or have the resources available to provide support to their students.

One of the many interesting aspects of this book is Fabienne's discussion around our understanding of the term 'Mental Health' and examining people's perceptions of language. It is really important to demystify what we mean by 'Mental Health' and help people to reframe their understanding. For example, the words 'stress' and 'anxiety' often have negative associations for people. However, stress is a natural response that is *meant* to make us feel uncomfortable, it happens to prompt us that something is wrong and we need to act on it. If a student is feeling stressed about an exam, what is causing that stress? Is it an uncertainty of what the exam will entail? Is it a concern over how to revise effectively, or is it a belief that exams are stressful events? This book will help you explore how, by examining the cause of the stress, rather than being afraid of the 'feeling' of the stress response, you can start to help students put a plan in place to reduce the stress.

Fabienne uses Einstein's quote that 'Change starts with you' in the book and for me this is really a key part of what this book is about. Similarly, in work with my own clients, the starting point is always to look at yourself. If you are in a good place psychologically, then you are much more able to be able to help other people. This book will aid you to reflect on where you are personally and your current understanding of your students' mental health. It will also guide you through working towards having the understanding, awareness and a practical toolbox to be able to help your students to do well and flourish.

I hope that you will get as much enjoyment from this book as I did and that it helps support your work.

Dr Anna Waters

Psychologist at Chimp Management Ltd

CONTENTS

INTRODUCTION

Welcome to *The Flourishing Student*

Are you an academic or professional member of staff in a Higher Education Institution?

Did you choose this profession because you saw it as an opportunity for sharing your passion for a subject or field with young people who will become the future workers, citizens and leaders?

Do you believe in making a positive contribution to young people's lives by helping your students to become culturally literate, intellectually reflective and committed to lifelong learning?

Are you keen to empower them to interact socially and respectfully with others and their communities and to possess all the core skills, competencies and habits required to become a confident and engaged adult, citizen and employee of the future?

Have you been wondering what is going on with young people, their mental health and well-being and why they are reporting increasing levels of stress and anxiety?

Have you had students come to your office, either very upset or despondent, indicating they felt that they could not achieve any or some of the things mentioned above?

Have you also been discussing your own level of stress and anxiety with your colleagues, finding yourself coping with a large amount of work, leaving at the end of each day feeling like you have not achieved all the tasks you had set for yourself?

If you answered yes to some of these questions then this book is for you.

What is the aim of this book?

When it comes to lecturing, teaching or helping our students, whilst we may hope for the perfect solution, or at least a formula that might help us make the best impact, sadly there is no magic wand.

This book is not about providing all the right answers around mental health in Higher Education or how to be a 'perfect academic tutor or member of staff in HE'. It's about how you, as a tutor, can help students to flourish not only academically but also in all aspects of their university lives, from a mental, emotional, physical, social and spiritual perspective. This book will show you how to be the best tutor you can be by understanding mental health and mental disorders, learning from students who have been able to thrive at university and to contribute to their communities. Best practice is shared all the time in the workplace so why aren't students given this opportunity?

This book will show how some students have used their personal experience and the interactions and relationships with their personal tutors as the first building block on their path to resilience, which is a building process: one brick at a time. Benard (2004, pp.3–4) defines resilience as 'a capacity all youth have for healthy development and successful learning' which should be seen not as a 'personality trait that one either has or does not have, rather than as an innate capacity bolstered by environmental protective factors' (p.9).

It most definitely is a journey with ups and downs for all who are part of this system. We all suffer from stress and anxiety. It's part of being human. Everything in life is transient. Our own lives are. I truly hope that this book shines a new light on the concept of mental health and well-being, and that it brings a new perspective that will make you not only reflect and ponder but also see how it can be directly applied to your life.

Why a book on mental health?

My own personal journey through emotions and challenges awoke in me a real passion for and interest in mental health and resilience, especially in education, which is the field I have been working in over the last 20 years.

Why a book on HE in particular?

I worked for two UK universities between 1998 and 2005. I then left for a period of ten years (to have children, and run my business). In 2014, I returned as an academic member of staff at the same UK university I left in 2005 and was taken aback by the changes I noticed. In less than ten years, students seemed less able to handle the academic work at university and less able to perform tasks that their peers could nine years ago. Their life and academic skills are clearly less developed than their predecessors. My tutees regularly report that their number one stressor is the academic workload, even though the workload has not increased.

As academic personal tutor, I see students from their first to their final year. My role is to provide academic support and to help them review some of their academic work, or develop their academic skills. I am often a 'listening ear' or the first person they come to see when they are experiencing personal and medical difficulties affecting their studies.

Since returning to higher education, I have also noticed the emphasis on mental health and mental health problems among students in higher education. The *Guardian* has a whole section on its website entitled 'Mental health: a university crisis'.[1] The media regularly report on this.

I am a trained Mindfulness teacher and a qualified hypnotherapist with a focus on stress and anxiety in education. My academic background is in linguistics and I became particularly interested in the linguistic use of mental health with negative modifiers and their impact on our understanding of this notion of mental health. I started reading articles and became intrigued by the notion of mental health crisis in education and decided to research this concept and interview experts in the field, as well as students who have been diagnosed with a mental disorder or are experiencing mental distress, and colleagues.

As part of this research, I came across Corey Keyes's (2002) concept of 'flourishing and languishing'. He describes the concept of *flourishing* as a life lived with high levels of emotional, psychological and social well-being (p.299). Flourishing individuals have enthusiasm for life, are productively engaged with others and in society, and are resilient in the face of personal challenges whereas a languishing individual is devoid of positive emotion towards life, is not functioning well psychologically or socially and has not been depressed in the past year (p.299). The interviews carried out with ten students from six different institutions throughout the UK and their stories of resilience suggest that there indeed is a difference between a *flourishing* and a *languishing* student and that it has an impact on their studies.

Over time, I have developed a new model to describe the *flourishing student*. The result of this work is the book you are reading. My wish is that you enjoy reading it as much as I enjoyed researching and writing it!

---

1   www.theguardian.com/education/series/mental-health-a-university-crisis [accessed 21/08/16].

What is this book about?

The aim of this book is threefold and will be split into three parts.

Overall, the focus is on bringing awareness, understanding and clarity around:

- the language and terminology used around terms such as mental health and well-being and how it affects our construct of these concepts
- the notion of the normal stresses of life versus mental disorder and illness
- the need for a new model that looks at students' experience holistically and not in parts
- the need for academics and professional members of staff in HE/FE who are non-specialists in this topic to become more aware of their own mental health and well-being but also how their work and contributions can have a positive impact on their student's university lives and experiences.

So, Part I will be looking at the language used around mental health and its association with negative words such as crisis, problems, issues and disorders. Does it have an impact on the way we perceive mental health, and mental-health issues? It will also focus on describing the differences between the normal response to daily life stresses and challenges and major mental illnesses. This section will demonstrate how they differ from 'normal negative mood disorders' created by life challenges such as bereavements, loss, illnesses, relationship issues, to name a few.

In Part II, we will look at the implication for education and the need for a new model that incorporates all the aspects that make a *flourishing student*. With the help of students' personal experiences, I will share the *flourishing student* model. This new model focuses on students' combined growth and development and focuses not solely on their mental health but on other aspects to see how it impacts on their university experience. It also highlights specific skills that a *flourishing student* seems to possess and provides the tutor with several tools to help students build a 'toolbox' to learn to flourish at university and to enjoy their studies and university life.

The last part of the book, Part III, will provide a more specific focus on practical activities that personal academic tutors can use to not only reflect on their own mental health, but also to help their tutees build their own 'toolkit' for self-management and resilience to better navigate the challenges and the ups and downs of university life more effectively.

Who is this book for?

It is aimed at anyone who would like to gain a deeper understanding of stress and anxiety among the student population in HE settings. It is specifically aimed at all academics and professional members of staff in Higher Education Institutions who are 'non-experts' on these topics and would like to gain clarity. This book will provide you with a clear understanding of the current research around mental health, the main issues experienced by students, how it affects them on a daily basis and, most importantly, how they engage in some self-care during the most challenging times. The latter part of this book will be particularly suited to academic personal tutors and will be filled with useful tips, practical activities and exercises that can be easily used and incorporated into individual or group tutoring sessions to help students develop their 'resilience toolbox'.

DISCLAIMER:

This book and the advice provided is NOT aimed at students who suffer from significant and long-term mental disorders or mental health problems which will all require specific professional and specialist treatments (see Chapter 2 for further details). If we take the analogy of a 'personal trainer', you will be providing your students with advice and tips on how to 'flourish' in terms of mental health, in the same way that a personal trainer would advise a client on how to become physically 'fitter' or to include exercises in their life to improve their physical health. But, just like a personal trainer would never tell their client what to do if they had a physical illness or a medical issue and would always advise them to consult a doctor, UNDER NO CIRCUMSTANCES should you ever provide medical advice to your students. Students who have mental disorders or who suffer from serious mental health problems should be referred to the relevant professionals so that they receive the mental health care most relevant and adapted to their needs. If in doubt, always talk to professionals and experts in the field of mental health and NEVER give information or advice that you are not trained to provide.

How to use this book

Unless you already have a great understanding and knowledge of stress and anxiety, mental health issues and disorders in HE settings, I would suggest that you start at the beginning of the book. The first two parts will enable you to gain a clear understanding of the situation, with a new model, which in turn will enable you to support your students even more effectively regardless of their level of study. The last part will provide you with practical skills and techniques to use during sessions with your personal tutees.

- PART I -

Gaining Understanding
and Clarity

Chapter 1
Setting the scene

The current state of student mental health in the UK's Higher Education

---

*'The noblest pleasure is the joy of understanding' –
Leonardo Da Vinci*

The general picture

To better understand the overall context surrounding the UK's HE, here are some facts that you might find interesting drawn from Universities UK.

- 2.3 million students were studying in the UK at HE level in 2015/16. It is in fact a slight decrease and is less than in 2010 when there were 2.5 million students registered at various British HE institutions.[2] But it most definitely is a lot more than in the early 1960s when

---

2   www.hesa.ac.uk/data-and-analysis/students.

only about one in 20 young people were going into higher education.

- 56.2% were female and 43.8% male.
- Almost 40% of them were aged 20 and under, 5.52% were aged between 25 and 30 and 11.3% aged 30 to 59.
- The majority study in England (1.87 million) then Scotland (218,400), Wales (125,680) and finally North-ern Ireland (52,650).
- Around 520,000 students lived in rented accommo-dation, 330,000 in accommodation maintained by the institutions, 327,000 lived at their parental/guard-ian home, 259,000 in their own accommodation and 118,000 in private sector halls.

What about student health?

The HE landscape – student epidemic or not… that is the question!

Mental health problems are a growing public health concern both in the UK and around the world. For example, the Mental Health Foundation states that around 12 million adults in the UK see their GP with mental health problems each year mostly for anxiety and depression and that one in four adults and one in ten children are likely to have a mental health problem in any year.[3]

Whether you have been working in the HE sector or not, I am sure you have become aware that over the last few years, the words 'mental health' and 'mental health problems' among stu-dents have been highlighted by the media. These articles have suggested that stress is much more prevalent than we think. A recent survey carried out by a private insurance company, in

---

3   www.mentalhealth.org.uk/sites/default/files/fundamental-facts-15.pdf

2013 entitled 'The Aviva Health of the Nation Index'[4] reported that a lot more of our GPs' time is spent dealing with mental health issues. It's the most prevalent type of illnesses, with 84% of GPs seeing more patients than ever before suffering from stress and anxiety. The conversations carried out with a GP working at a Student Health Service confirmed this and they described their work as 'trying to close the stable door after the horse has bolted'.

In 2013, the National Union of Students (NUS) published a survey of 1,200 students entitled 'Mental Distress Survey',[5] of which 92% of respondents identified as having had feelings of mental distress, which often includes feeling down, stressed and demotivated. On average, respondents who experience feelings of mental distress experience them once a month or more (74%), and almost one third suffered mental distress every week.

The main causes provided were:

1. coursework for 65% of respondents
2. exams and study (54%)
3. financial difficulty (47%).

'CRI66', the report by the Royal College of Psychiatrists entitled *Mental Health of Students in Higher Education* published in January 2011 also provides insight into the research carried out around the mental health issues encountered by students. Bewick et al. (2008) carried out an Internet-based survey of mental distress in students in four UK Higher Education Institutions and found that 29% of students described clinical levels of psychological distress.

---

4   www.aviva.co.uk/library/pdfs/health/hotn-spring-2012-gen4421.pdf
5   www.nus.org.uk/Global/Campaigns/20130517%20Mental%20 Distress%20Survey%20%20Overview.pdf

When I first started researching this topic and saw these figures, I was convinced that there was a real 'crisis' and that an increasing number of students were suffering from mental health 'issues'.

Research has clearly shown that many of the major mental illnesses begin to appear during adolescence and early adulthood, so it is important to not only bring awareness to mental health and mental illnesses/disorders but also a clear understanding of what constitutes a mental disorder/illness so that everyone in education (staff, parents and students alike) has the right knowledge, competences and attitudes not only to help themselves, but also others, if need be.

What I didn't immediately notice, however, was that newspapers are using surveys and data which don't differentiate between self-reported and epidemiological data drawn from longitudinal cross-section studies for example or randomized control trials.

The interviews carried out with stress and anxiety specialists such as GPs, and practising counselling psychotherapists in the UK, Canada and the US made me aware of this fact and presented a different side to the coin which seemed to challenge the current narratives that mental health problems are massively increasing. According to several research studies (McMartin et al. 2014; Baxter 2014) on the epidemiological data over the last 50 years, it would appear that the incidence of mental health problems globally has remained steady.

Baxter (2014) recently tested the statements that common mental disorders have become more prevalent over the past two decades and found no evidence for an increased prevalence of anxiety disorders or Major Depressive Disorders (MDD). For example, the prevalence of anxiety disorders was estimated at 3.8% in 1990 and 4.0% in 2010. The prevalence of MDD was unchanged at 4.4% in 1990 and 2010. In his study whilst the crude number of cases increased by 36%, this can be explained by population growth previously mentioned and changing age structures.

The stark contrast, however, is that eight of the 11 General Health Questionnaire studies found a significant increase in psychological distress over time.

The conclusion is that the perceived 'epidemic' of common mental disorders is most likely explained by the increasing numbers of affected patients driven by increasing population sizes. Additional factors that may explain this perception include the higher rates of psychological distress as measured using symptom checklists, greater public awareness and the use of terms such as anxiety and depression in a context where they do not represent clinical disorders. (There will be more on this in Chapter 2 when we look at the different stages of mental health.)

McMartin et al. (2014) also decided to investigate trends in the prevalence of symptoms of mental health in a large population-based cohort of Canadian children and adolescents because they felt that existing research and media reports conveyed conflicting impressions of such trends.

They concluded that with the exception of hyperactivity, the prevalence of symptoms of mental illness in Canadian children and adolescents has remained relatively stable from 1994/95 to date. They also suggested that conflicting reports of escalating rates of mental illness in Canada may be explained by differing methodologies between studies, and increase in treatment.

Based on all the above information, what becomes significantly noticeable is the fact that the self-report of depressive symptoms/stress clearly has increased over time.

What might create the notion of increase in severity of anxiety, and stress in students across the world?

If we take a look at the various surveys and data mentioned in the first part of this section, it is obvious that they are based on self-reported symptoms. This is not to say that these symptoms are not real – far from it. I have no doubt that students are experiencing and showing signs of distress.

But when a researcher and non-expert in the field ask students questions such as 'In the last six months have you felt depressed or anxious?', participants tick yes and this creates the basis of self-reported data.

Based on this, the question we should therefore be asking is not: who is wrong or who is right in this debate, but to recognize that there IS a crisis of vulnerability and anxiety about having mental health problems among young people and students in education.

But instead of focusing on this 'crisis' it might be more productive to view it from a different perspective and to tackle this topic differently than we have done thus far.

Why are students reporting getting increasingly stressed?

The general labelling found in the media of university as being the best time of students' lives may not be true for every student.

When I interviewed students, it became clear that many of them experience a real period of transition when they move to a new city and join a university for the first year of their degree. It is a transition between adolescence and adulthood. It is also a transition between dependence and independence, in a new environment, away from the safety and security of home. They consider the staff members in the departments/schools where they study as their main points of contact. They rely on us as adults to provide them with advice and guidance.

The 'CR166' report by the Royal College of Psychiatrists (2011) agrees with this statement too and recognizes that 'Students are at a stage of transition between dependence and independence. Many have to cope with the stresses of moving from home to university at an age when they are negotiating significant developmental stages' (p.18).

Have you ever wondered why so many of our students say that they are feeling stressed?

A lot of research is currently being carried out to understand the reasons behind this increased self-reported stress and anxiety among students. It is a rather complex and multifaceted issue and there is no single answer. One student I interviewed summarized it beautifully when she said:

> There are problems everywhere. It's a generation issue – where we are surrounded by problems with the media telling us that we should all be slimmer and what diet to follow – what degree to do to earn a lot of money, what to look like and how to succeed and even how to choose a boyfriend. Your job and your career says everything about you. It's not the same values as one or two generations before. As a result, when you go to university, you are not just there to study, you are there to make friends, to be popular, to be known and so if those aren't happening, you question yourself.

This statement clearly highlights the complexity of the issue and all the challenges, not only academic but also personal and social, that students are faced with when they join a HE institution and embark on their degree.

Below is a list of some of the specific points highlighted by students in previous research and drawn from my own interviews:

- Academic workload – many of my students regularly state that their number one stress is the workload. Research also seems to confirm this with large studies of the major stressors of the first year indicating that they cannot handle the academic work of university (Sax 1997). Yet, this workload has not changed and is not more demanding than in previous years.

- Concerns about the future – the 'doom and gloom' stories in the press, and social media about Brexit and Donald Trump for example. The uncertainty and the fear of something going wrong in the future. This will all contribute to the automatic nervous system kicking in (we will see more about this in Chapter 2 about stress).

- Exams and assessments. A survey called 'Silently Stressed' carried out by NUS Scotland found that 90% of 1,800 students from 19 FE colleges and 15 universities across Scotland reported that exams and assessments caused them more stress than anticipated and only 2% said they experienced no stress at all.[6] This reported stress means that some of my tutees are unable to revise and they procrastinate and leave their work until the last minute, which creates even more stress for them as they get nearer the deadline and realize they will not be able to meet it.

- Extrinsic instead of intrinsic motivation. Several students mentioned the fact that they felt that they had chosen to come to university for 'extrinsic' reasons and that they were motivated to come to university to earn their degree (with a good classification) so that they could get a good job which is well paid and would help them to lead a comfortable life. One student in particular said to me 'I am in my final year so I am not going to stop now but after having therapy and discussing my

---

6   www.nus.org.uk/PageFiles/12238/THINK-POS-REPORT-Final.pdf

situation, I now realize that I shouldn't have come to university because I didn't have enough intrinsic motivation or an internal desire to engage and participate in university life fully because I found it personally rewarding or enjoyable. I did because that's what my parents and teachers expected from me and encouraged me to do and I didn't want to upset them. I was also worried that I would not be able to find a job otherwise.' He added 'Society says that young people need a degree to get a good job, earn good money and be happy but I am not sure that's true.'

Of course, this is not suggesting that all students feel this way or that extrinsic motivation is bad as it can be beneficial in some situations. We will discuss the balance between intrinsic and extrinsic motivation further in Chapter 4 of the book.

- Financial worries. The increase in university fees and financial worries has featured regularly in the press. Students regularly mention the fact that they must pay £9,000 per year to attend university.

  The impact of financial concerns on overall mental health has become a popular topic among researchers and practitioners. For example, Roberts et al. (2000) identified a link between adverse financial situations of college students and the negative impact on mental and physical health that translated into mental distress. Andrews and Wilding (2004) found that financial stressors were positively associated with increased anxiety and depression levels among college students in the United Kingdom.

- Future careers. In the same survey, over 75% of students reported that considering their future career prospects after graduation was reasonably or very stressful. Some students I interviewed said that it was linked to the pressure they feel about their exams and assessments, as they believe that they must perform and achieve to get the best job possible when they leave university. These feelings are also increased by stories in the media, which suggest that there are specific degrees that will help students to earn the largest amounts of money.

- Poor diet/reduced physical activity. We will see in Part II how important our physical health is for our overall well-being. Students I spoke to as part of our research highlighted the fact that they felt much better after doing some sport (as part of the numerous clubs offered in their institution) or if they went for a walk or a run. There is a growing body of evidence indicating that physical activity and fitness can benefit both the health and academic performance of students. Eating a healthy and balanced diet, which includes raw fruits, and fresh vegetables, for example, has long been known to be good for our health. Jacka et al.'s study (2011) confirms this and highlights the fact that there have been a number of published studies identifying an inverse association between diet quality and the common mental disorders, depression and anxiety, in adults. They also confirm the importance of diet in adolescence and its potential role in modifying mental health over the life course.

- Pressure to perform – get a 2:1 or a first. Students put a lot of pressure on themselves and have high expectations. They want to succeed and they think that it is important to gain a 2:1 or a first so that they can get a good job that pays well at the end of their studies and clear their debts. This is obvious for us as academic members of staff when we provide students with feedback or discuss points about exams as many students seem to be mainly driven and motivated by the mark rather than the feedback which will help them to improve and progress.

- Relationship difficulties. Some of the students I interviewed explained that whilst they mostly enjoy their relationships with their parents, friends, flatmates or their boyfriends/girlfriends, at times these relationships created some stress and anxiety because they sometimes 'went wrong'. Neff and Karney's (2009) study confirmed the common wisdom that the greater the stress in our lives, the more reactive we are to the normal ups and downs of our relationship. They explain that relationships exposed to high stress for a long amount of time are bound to falter. During such times, we are more likely to see the relationship as being negative, not realizing the impact the stress is having on the validity of our evaluation – it colours our perception of the relationship itself. Remove the stress, and people's positive relationship skills can once again – and usually do – take over.

- Social media and use of technology. Social media and the use of technology have clearly improved our lives and have enabled us to connect with people on the other side of the planet. The Internet enables us to get information almost instantly and to raise awareness of political, and social issues. In many ways, it has brought very positive things in our lives but we also tend to spend a lot of time on social media or connected via our phones and other electronic gadgets. Have you ever downloaded an app to see how much time you spend on your phone, or surfing the net? I did and got so horrified that I quickly deleted the app. (If you want to find out for yourself check out https://inthemoment.io/, for example).

  According to a study conducted by the Kaiser Family Foundation (Rideout et al. 2010) teenagers on average reportedly spend up to 7.5 hours on media per day. This suggests that young people are highly connected and that they engage in a high level of new-technology mediated interactions (both for learning and social activities).

Work recently carried out by researchers show that social media and being constantly connected also has a negative impact on our lives ranging from insomnia to depression. For example, Fardouly et al. (2015) carried out a study which experimentally investigated the effect of Facebook usage on women's mood and body image, and whether these effects differ from reading an online fashion magazine. The findings were that participants who spent time on Facebook reported being in a more negative mood than those who spent time on the online fashion magazine. Furthermore, women high in appearance comparison tendency reported more facial, hair and skin-related discrepancies after Facebook exposure than exposure to the control website. A student I interviewed said that he had to delete Facebook from his phone and computer because he had become addicted and spent too much time checking his newsfeed/comments about his status. He also said that he worried about what others thought of his pictures and his comments and regularly had to ask friends to comment or like his pictures to help him feel less self-conscious.

- Substance misuse. Some students I interviewed reported using some substances excessively to get through the day (drugs but also alcohol, caffeine supplements, prescription drugs as well as energy drinks). Bennett and Holloway (2013) showed that drug misuse on the university campus was widespread in terms of the types and patterns of misuse. The most troublesome findings concern the high levels of multiple drug use, including some of the most dangerous drugs (e.g. crack and powder cocaine and heroin, as well as ketamine) and the list of recorded harms experienced as a result of this. They conclude that little attention has been paid outside the United States to drug consumption among university students or to interventions designed to prevent it. There are signs in the United Kingdom that government policy is beginning to pay attention to these specific drug problems among university students. I will show in Part II that drugs can have a big and negative impact on a student's physical health and is therefore important to the concept of the 'flourishing student'.

- The impact of overparenting also known as helicopter parenting and high parental expectations (Cline and Fay 1990; Munich and Munich 2009). This topic has drawn the attention of both the popular media and researchers over the last few years. This phenomenon involves the application of developmentally inappropriate parenting such as the use of excessive advice, problem solving and provision of abundant and unnecessary tangible assistance combined with risk aversion, anxiety and parental involvement in the child's emotional well-being to the point of enmeshment (Segrin et al. 2012). These parenting practices reduce demands on children to undertake behaviours that would effect change in their own lives (Locke et al. 2012). The main issue with helicopter parenting is that it does not teach students to learn from their mistakes and to become independent. As a result, there is an increased attitude from some students who simply say: 'I can't do it, do it for me.'

- Transition from secondary school to university and issues of coping with independent living and life at university. Hughes (2012) explains that transition to higher education can be a stressful experience, often resulting in psychological distress, anxiety, depression, sleep disturbance, reduction in self-esteem and isolation. He also adds that transition has been found to play a key role in student suicide.

According to Richardson et al. (2012) the first year of university study is one of the greatest transition periods in a student's life. It is a time where they must learn new academic skills as well as new social and independent living skills. For many students, the struggle to balance the competing demands of study, work and personal commitments feels overwhelming and they report significant declines in their overall health and well-being.

Some of the students I interviewed also clearly stated that they found their experience at university challenging because they didn't feel they had the skills required to tackle some of the tasks set in their first year at university. Listening to their stories, it would appear that some students have difficulties dealing with the academic workload because it is so different from what they are asked to achieve for their A levels where their work is being 'chunked down' into 'bite-size bits' that they 'digest' and 'regurgitate' to get the grades they need for their GCSE and A levels. Students explained that their tutors were there 'every step of the way' and that they were always told 'what to do next'. This is clearly required by secondary schools (and more and more primary schools) because of the pressure on members of staff (who have performance-related pay) and schools (for funding) to ensure that as many students as possible get good grades.

The issues with our language uses of the words 'mental health'

As a linguist, I love words and definitions. This is particularly true of the English words I had to learn as a second foreign language because they sometimes differ so much from my mother tongue. When I developed an interest in stress, anxiety and resilience, I started reading articles in the press and analysed the words used. What struck me the most was that the word 'mental health', which would be translated as *'santé mentale'* in French and implies 'health of the mind' or 'wellness of the mind' was associated with negative words such as issues, problems, ill-health, illness or even disorders. These words were used intermittently and interchangeably. When I discussed this concept with a colleague, they told me that in Spanish *'salud mental'* also has positive connotations, as something good you are doing for your own mind.

This was rather surprising because I also thought and felt that there was a difference between an issue, a problem and a disorder. As a result, 'mental health' seems to have a loaded meaning that the words 'physical health' or 'social health' do not seem to contain.

In *The structure of magic I* Bandler and Grinder (1975) explain that 'when humans communicate – when we talk, discuss, write – we usually are not conscious of the process of selecting words to represent our experience'. This is obviously a good thing as otherwise it would impact on our exchanges with people if we had to think about every single word we use when we speak. However, they also state that thus:

> we are almost never conscious of the way in which we order and structure the words we select. Language so fills our world that we move through it as a fish swims through water (1975, p.22).

Could this lack of conscious awareness of language selection lead us to simply accept word collocations and not to question them? Could this unconsciously impact on our definitions and acceptance of such collocations?

To answer this question, let's first look up all the various definitions of these words.

Mental health... a definition

'Mental health' is a mass noun and the Oxford Dictionary describes it as 'a person's condition with regard to their psychological and emotional well-being'.

Mental health was defined by the World Health Organization (WHO) as a 'state of well-being in which every individual realizes his or her own potential, can cope with the normal stresses of life, can work productively and fruitfully, and is able to make a contribution to her or his community' (WHO 2004).

Mental health is, according to the Surgeon General (US Office of the Surgeon General 2001, p.4), 'a state of successful performance of mental function, resulting in productive activities, fulfilling relationships with people, and the ability to change and cope with adversity'.

Once more, the above definitions brought up many questions for me as a linguist. You will no doubt agree with me that it is a very positive and empowering definition.

So, why are we not seeing it used in the press and media more often, with that positive sense of 'state of well-being' just like we see the word physical health on its own as meaning a 'state of physical well-being'?

How can we explain the discrepancies between these positive definitions and the loaded and negative connotation the world 'mental health' currently holds? Is it solely because of the use of the negative modifiers alongside it? Why are we using negative modifiers with such a positively charged word? Why are we not provided with the positive definitions more often as it seems so much more empowering?

Is the use of these modifiers nonsensical if we use 'state of well-being' instead of 'mental health' (i.e. 'state of well-being issue', 'state of well-being problem', 'state of well-being disorder')?

The confusing impact of multiple negative modifiers

To try and answer all these questions, we need to first look at the differences between the various modifiers associated with 'mental health'.

These are used regularly in the press and during our conversations:

Mental health condition	Mental illness	Mental health disorder
Mental health issue	Mental health crisis	Mental health problem
Mental health illness	Mental ill health	Mental disorder

Confused already? So was I when I first started researching the topic of 'mental health'.

There are many modifiers collocated with mental health including 'crisis', 'issues', 'disorders' and 'problems'. What we can notice is that all of the words listed carry negative connotations that seem to reinforce the 'wrongness' and the 'badness' of what is associated with the state of one's mind. All these expressions are also used intermittently and interchangeably as meaning the same thing, thus creating semantic confusion. When young people and non-experts in the field use the language, they are now confusing 'mental health' with 'mental disorder'.

It is vital to bring back some clarity around the linguistic uses of 'mental health' because as George Orwell pointed out in his essay 'Politics and the English Language' (1946), 'the English language becomes ugly and inaccurate since our thoughts are foolish, but the slovenliness of our language makes it easier for us to have foolish thoughts.'

We need to pay more attention to the words we use when we talk about mental health because a muddled language will lead to muddled thinking.

But as Orwell also explains this process is reversible and even though:

> Modern English, especially written English, is full of bad habits which spread by imitation it can be avoided if one is willing to take the necessary trouble. If one gets rid of these habits one can think more clearly.

Why so much negativity?

The use of these negative modifiers suggests that negative information tends to influence evaluations more strongly than comparably positive information around the topic of 'mental health'.

Cacioppo et al. (1997) describe it as 'negativity bias'. In one of his studies, Cacioppo showed undergraduate students pictures known to generate positive feelings (for example a pizza or a fast car), those certain to arouse negative feelings (a mutilated face or dead cat) and those known to stir up neutral feelings (a plate, a hairdryer). He also recorded the electrical activity in the participant's cerebral cortex that highlights the amount of information processing taking place.

His conclusions were that our brains demonstrate more responsivity to negative stimuli than positive stimuli. Negative stimuli generate a greater surge in electrical activity. As a result, our attitudes and behaviours are more strongly influenced by negative input than positive input (Cacioppo et al. 1994).

Cacioppo also suggests that the negative bias is introduced at the response output stage and coincides with Cannon's (1929) notion that threatening stimuli are more likely to elicit general and diffuse sympathetic activation as part of an adaptive fight or flight response which emphasizes the relative impact of negative information on our actions. Although the term 'fight or flight' was coined three-quarters of a century ago, the legacy of Cannon's phrase is still obvious and present in the culture at large and has clearly helped us understand the human stress response. The negativity bias could therefore be treated as an inherent characteristic of the negative motivational structure in the central nervous system (Cacioppo et al. 1997; Cacioppo et al. 1994). In order to keep us safe, our nervous system has therefore designed ways to make it impossible for us to miss possible dangers and threats and therefore respond to it.

We will see how important and relevant this concept is when we discuss the 'fight or flight response' in Chapter 2.

The modifiers used with 'mental health' invariably carry an unpleasant and threatening connotation and as such enter in the reader's 'emotional memory' or 'implicit memory' as Le-Doux (1998) and Kihlstrom et al. (2000) explain, and exercise tremendous impact on future behaviour by way of fear conditioning. This may explain why these negative modifiers are used so commonly and regularly in the press and by the general public.

Rozin and Royzman (2001) also consider the contagiousness of negative events as the primary reason for their strength and dominance. This may explain why there has been such a rise in the reports of stress and anxiety suggesting a 'crisis in mental health in HE'. The student responses during our interviews seem to corroborate this concept, as students stated that reading articles or hearing stories of other people having a difficult time and being stressed made them much more aware of their own problems. This left them with the feeling that 'yes, that's me. I think I am also experiencing these issues or this extreme level of stress.'

The semantic confusion created by the interchanging use of negative modifiers such as 'disorder', 'crisis', 'issue', 'problem' collocated to the phrase mental health means that we start believing that we can substitute one modifier for the other and still convey the same meaning.

For example, what is a mental health disorder? If mental health means 'state of well-being' – would it make any sense for me to say there is a 'state of well-being disorder' in young people or 'a state of well-being crisis in education'?

Language is obviously a vital tool. Not only does it help us communicate our thoughts, and ideas but it also helps us connect with others and create cultural ties, friendships and relationships. Language enables not only the expression of thoughts, emotions, perceptions and feelings but it also empowers us to express our values and our social identity. So, let's see why the language we use around mental health matters, starting with a bit of history to assess how the concept of mental health has evolved over the years. We will then tackle the specific language uses around mental health in Chapter 2.

The language we use matters

A little bit of history

Ancient treatments of psychological disorders were inhuman and included exorcism, being caged like animals and being beaten, for example. It took a long time to think that mental health was not simply a 'sickness of the mind'.

Philippe Pinel (1745–1826) was a French physician who pioneered the humane treatment of the mentally ill. He insisted that madness was not due to demonic possession, but an ailment of the mind.

In 1886, 'Nellie Bly', the pen name of Elizabeth Jane Cochrane, was trying to establish herself as an investigative journalist on the *New York World* when she was asked if she could have herself committed to one of the asylums for the insane in New York, with a view to writing a narrative of the treatment of the patients therein and the methods of management. So, she did and feigned a mental illness to report on the truly awful conditions in the US inside psychiatric hospitals known as 'asylums'. She found rotten food, cold showers, rats, abusive nurses and patients being tied down. She also called 'the insane asylum on Blackwell's Island a human rat-trap where it is easy to get in, but once there it is impossible to get out'.

After her ten days, she wrote a series of revelatory news articles in the *World*, causing an uproar. The following year, she rewrote the articles in the form of a short book, *Ten Days in a Mad-House*. This 'plain and unvarnished' writing makes fascinating reading of what had been standard mental health treatments for centuries. Her work led the charge to mental health reform and the way mental disorders were seen.

The introduction of the medical model

When physicians discovered that syphilis led to mental disorders and could manifest in serious neurological problems like dementia, irritability and various mental disorders, their perspective began to shift to the medical model of psychological disorder that supports the idea that psychological disorders have physiological causes that can be diagnosed based on symptoms. This was an important step forward. So, eventually a lot of those so-called 'mental patients' were removed from asylums and moved to hospitals so that all of their symptoms could be treated and even cured. The medical models started being used to review the physical causes of these disorders. It also enabled people who observed the 'patient' to notice some 'signs', which could be indicative of a mental disorder.

This new way of thinking was an important step forward, at least at first because it took us past this habit of simply locking people up when they didn't seem quite right to others. It also encouraged us to start using specific vocabulary that would enable us to not only understand but also define mental disorders with an attempt at the use of a common language.

The importance of standards and measures

An important factor for professionals and specialists of mental health as well as for patients is attempting to standardize and measure mental disorders. How we talk about them, diagnose them and treat them.

In an attempt to do so, specialists created a manual to classify psychological disorders. The American Psychiatric Association (2013) published a *Diagnostic and statistical manual of mental disorders (DSM)* to describe psychological disorders. The most recent edition is *DSM-5* and is designed to be work in progress forever as each new edition incorporates the latest research and how our understanding of mental health and behaviour evolves over time. For example, in the first two editions, homosexuality was classified as a pathology. It was eliminated in 1973 as a reflection of changing attitudes and understanding of sexual orientations.

The *DSM* functionally defines mental illnesses in the United States but also in the UK and other countries. It is used by practically everybody (from clinicians, insurance and drug companies, to policymakers and the legal system). But in 2013, not everyone accepted the new version of the *DSM-5*.

In a statement, Thomas R. Insel (2013), the then MD of the National Institute of Mental Health, the world's largest funding agency for research into mental health, indicated that it was withdrawing its support of the manual.

Insel stated that:

> the goal of this new manual, as with all previous editions, is to provide a common language for describing psychopathology. While DSM has been described as a "Bible" for the field, it is, at best, a dictionary, creating a set of labels and defining each. The strength of each of the editions of DSM has been "reliability" – each edition has ensured that clinicians use

the same terms in the same ways. The weakness is its lack of validity. Patients with mental disorders deserve better.

Labelling psychological disorders

Labels may be helpful for health-care professionals when communicating with one another and establishing therapy but as we have seen critics argue that labels may stigmatize individuals.

In 1973, American psychologist David Rosenhan from Stanford University published a paper entitled 'On being sane in insane places', detailing an experiment he carried out on psychiatric institutions themselves. Between 1969 and 1972, Rosenhan himself and a group of colleagues, gained admission to psychiatric hospitals by simulating and faking a single symptom – by complaining that they had been hearing voices. Asked what the voices said, they replied that they were often unclear, but as far as they could tell they said 'empty', 'hollow', and 'thud'. The voices were unfamiliar and were of the same sex as the pseudo patient. The moment they were admitted into hospital, they abandoned the symptoms and behaved the way they normally did. Their question was: would anyone detect that they were sane? The answer: no. They never did – they were all given a diagnostic of paranoid schizophrenia and released with the diagnostic of 'paranoid schizophrenia in remission'.

For Rosenhan, 'in remission' doesn't mean quite the same thing as 'sane'. He describes his experience in the psychiatric hospitals as 'dehumanised' where nobody talks to you and nobody has contact with you. On average, the staff talked to patients for 6.5 minutes a day and there were not many visits. Rosenhan was on a ward with 41 men and his wife constituted four of the seven visitors at a weekend. He described psychiatric hospitals as:

store houses in society for people who you really don't want, really don't understand and for whom you have lost a great deal of sympathy. Staff needed to be constantly reminded that although they are doing the best they can at the fore-front, people are not merely collections of symptoms, they are people with spouses, children, parents, jobs and mort-gages to pay but are in the fuller sense very human and very unhappy. (Rosenhan 1973)

Another of Rosenhan's criticisms of the institutions is that they viewed mental illness as an irreversible condition, almost like a personality trait rather than a curable illness. Labelling in psy-chiatric assessment plays an important role. Having once been labelled schizophrenic, there is nothing the pseudo patient can do to overcome the tag. 'The tag profoundly colors others' per-ceptions of him and his behaviour', he said.

Rosenhan's work has been criticized but it raised questions such as how do we define, diagnose and classify mental disor-der? And at what point does 'sad' become 'depressed' or 'ener-getic' 'hyperactive' or 'anxious' a 'disorder'? What are the risks and benefits of diagnostics and labelling and how does the field keep evolving? When we think about mental disorders, we also often link them to psychology, psychiatry and to the condi-tions they have been created to understand, diagnose and treat, that is, the mental illnesses and disorders ranging from com-mon disorders that some of us will experience to more serious conditions that require more care.

Mental health workers view mental disorders as persistent-ly harmful thoughts, feelings and actions. When behaviour is deviant, distressful and dysfunctional psychiatrists and psy-chologists label it *disordered* (Comer 2004). This definition contains sensitive words such as deviant – thoughts and be-haviours that are different from the rest of the cultural con-text. For example, walking naked outside in the street in one culture may be considered normal, while in others it may lead to the person being arrested. Deviant behaviour must accompany distress to be considered a disorder. Distressful means a subjective feeling that something is really wrong which in turn leads to dysfunction when a person's ability to work and live is clearly often measurably impaired.

The danger of labelling oneself and others

Have you ever heard a joke about someone having cancer or made a casual reference to someone having high blood pressure; have you ever teased anyone by saying that he's got diabetes? Of course not, because we don't tend to make fun of someone for having a physical illness. In fact, we tend to have a lot of empathy for people when they are 'physically' unwell or ill. But in our society, some people make comments about others having 'mental illnesses' and never give it a second thought. Have you ever used or heard someone refer to somebody else as a 'psycho', 'schizo' or 'bipolar' or even that he or she is 'mental' or 'OCD'? As previously mentioned, when we use these words, we tend to do so almost automatically and without having a full understanding of their meaning but this has a significant impact on how we perceive 'mental health' and 'mental disorders' and it increases the stigma around these topics. By using these words with the verb 'to be', we give people who experience them an identity or a label. The problem with identities and labels is that they can lead to a feeling that it is something permanent and as one student indicated 'that we may be stuck with' for the rest of our lives.

A number of studies have been published which confirm this idea. For example, in their 2014 article 'The far-reaching effects of believing people can change', Yeager et al. look at the belief that personality is fixed (called an *entity theory* of personality) and how it can give rise to negative reactions to social adversities. Their three studies demonstrated that when social adversity is common – at the transition to high school – an entity theory can affect overall stress, health and achievement. Study 1 showed that an entity theory of personality, measured during the first month of 9th grade, predicted more negative immediate reactions to social adversity, and at the end of the year, greater stress, poorer health and lower grades. Studies 2 and 3 tested a brief intervention that taught a malleable (incremental) theory of personality – the belief that people can change. The incremental theory group showed less negative reactions to an immediate experience of social adversity and eight months later, reported lower overall stress and physical illness. They also achieved better academic performance over the year.

Their conclusion is that it is important to challenge the common idea in our societies that being labelled 'cool' or a 'nerd' early in high school defines a person forever after, regardless of the changes they may make later. Their research clearly shows that adolescents can learn to tell themselves a different story, a story in which people have the potential to change. When they do, they show better adjustment across the board: lower stress, better health and higher grades. They finish by saying that 'going forward, it will be important for researchers, educators, parents, and media outlets to find ways to emphasize this message of human potential for change'.

The study by Rosenthal and Jacobson detailed in 'Pygmalion in the classroom' (1968) seem to also strengthen this idea. The authors conducted an experiment in a public elementary school, telling teachers that certain children could be expected to be 'growth spurters', based on the students' results on the Harvard Test of Inflected Acquisition. But in fact, the test was non-existent and those children designated as 'spurters' were chosen at random. What Rosenthal and Jacobson hoped to determine by this experiment was the degree (if any) to which changes in teacher expectation produce changes in student achievement. The results of this experiment provide further evidence that one person's expectations of another's behaviour may come to serve as a self-fulfilling prophecy. When teachers expected that certain children would show greater intellectual development, those children did show greater intellectual development. Once again, we can see what the implications would be for mental health and how what we believe about our students may have an impact on the way they perform or achieve.

The difference between behaviour and identity

In Neuro Linguistic Programming (NLP), we draw a difference between our behaviour (what we do and say, how we behave) and our identity (who we are). Our behaviours do not define who we are and the danger with calling someone a 'psycho' or a 'schizo' is that it suggests it is something they cannot change. It is a label that will be with them forever. It is much more difficult to change who you are than how you behave.

When I studied NLP, I came across Robert Dilts' 'Neuro-logical levels of change', first laid out in his book *Changing Belief Systems with NLP* (1990). Dilts identifies six different levels of experience corresponding to six different levels of neurological 'circuitry' or 'thinking' that makes up our experiences in life.

They take the shape of a pyramid with environment at the bottom and spirituality at the top.

- Purpose (spirituality) – what is my intention and purpose?
- Identity – who am I?
- Beliefs and values – what are our beliefs? What is important to us?

- Capabilities – what am I capable of?
- Behaviour – how do we behave and how should we behave?
- Environment – in what context does the behaviour occur?

We will discuss the implication of these levels further in Chapter 4 but it is extremely important to link 'behaviour' and 'identity' to the discussion here. When I talked to students, there seemed to be a clear confusion where students mistook their behaviour – what they do when they are upset or what is happening in a particular environment – for who they are and their identity. As we have seen before, there is a big difference between what we do and who we are and if we start 'confusing' one for the other or 'labelling' ourselves as 'depressed' or 'stressed', it will be much more difficult to remove this label. For example, one student told me that 'he was feeling upset because his grandmother died and that as a result he was depressed'. This example highlights the fact that we use the terminology 'I am depressed' to talk about a sad event or a sad feeling we experience (here the death of a close relative) but this does not mean that we 'are depressed' or more exactly that we suffer from depression, but that we are experiencing grief and sadness at the loss of a family member whom we loved dearly.

Here is another example that I hope will show the difference between behaviour and identity. Imagine that you have a student who is enjoying studying, is engaged and learning. They are working hard, studying, doing their homework. For intrinsic reasons, the student is motivated to undertake the task for the sake of it only and not because they are gaining good marks but as a result of the work and the effort they put in, they are doing well academically and are getting good marks. As teachers and parents, we would of course be proud of their 'behaviour' and what they are doing. But very often, instead of saying so: 'I can see how hard you are working', or 'I can see you are doing well', we tend to automatically move up to the identity level and say 'how clever are you', 'you are so bright', 'you are so intelligent', 'I can see how academically minded you are and how good you are at studying'.

This would have a very damaging effect (and we will see again why in Part III) because if the student studying changes their 'behaviour' and stops working as hard, their marks and their learning might decrease. This would probably then lead some of the students to change their identity and to suddenly believe that 'they are not clever enough'. This has been confirmed several times by my tutees who got a 2:2 mark when they first started university and who came to see me in floods of tears because they believed that 'they were not clever enough to be studying here'. One can clearly see or understand how upsetting for a student it would be if they have been labelled 'clever', 'bright', 'intelligent' in primary and secondary school because they got straight As or A*s and how they could then easily mistake their 2:2 mark for an indication of how 'incapable' they are. It is easier to change what we do than to change who we are, our identity which is at the core of our 'persona'. As personal tutors and members of staff at the university, it is important for us to be aware of the language we use when we talk to students in order to avoid 'strengthening' or 'anchoring' the belief that a student's behaviour defines who they are.

Becoming aware of the stigma around mental health

Despite all the progress made around mental health, most of us have at some point in our life stigmatized or had thoughts or attitudes that discriminated against others. For example, in the English language words such as 'he is mental' are often used to describe someone who is behaving in a silly way for attention or in a random, sporadic way, involving nonsensical referenc-

es and actions that usually result in general amusement and
hilarity of the onlookers. The key point here is to recognize
that these words and thoughts are part of our vocabulary and
attitudes. However, it is also important to analyse their origin
and to challenge them by recognizing what effect they have on
others, how they impact on the way we conceive mental health
and mental disorders and how they contribute to the stigma
surrounding mental health. In Greek and Latin, a stigma was a
mark or a brand, especially one that marked a slave, so a stigma
marked a person as inferior. When stigma began to be used
in the English language, it usually meant the kind of mark or
stain you can't actually see. We use the word stigma to describe
misconceptions and incorrect beliefs around mental disorders
and illnesses and it is important to challenge them.

According to Corrigan (2000) and Pen and Martin (1998)
the general public seems to infer mental illness from four cues:
psychiatric symptoms, social-skills deficits, physical appearance and labels. Research suggests that stigma may impede
people from seeking or fully participating in mental health
services. The threat of social disapproval or diminished self-esteem that accompanies the label may account for underused
services (Corrigan 2004). It is therefore important that we pay
attention to the words we use around mental health so that we
influence how it is perceived, help reduce the stigma and help
those who need it to seek and participate in the treatment they
require.

Several of the students I interviewed used the word 'stigma' to express how they felt about their personal situation and
made comments such as 'there is stigma out there – it's a private thing – I don't want people to know it's me – don't want to
be recognized.' 'Stigma around mental health – mental health
is really misunderstood, I felt really misunderstood and lonely
before I was diagnosed and before I opened up and shared with
my friends and family.'

The other issue lies with some of our vocabulary used to describe how we feel on a daily basis. If we use expressions such 'anxiety' as meaning 'anxiety disorder' or 'depressed' as meaning 'clinical depression' or 'stress' as meaning 'chronic stress', we create semantic confusion between a normal response to an external stressor and a mental disorder. We will see in Part II that there is indeed a difference between 'stress' and 'chronic stress', for example. One of the problems is that when young people are using this language to describe their mental health, they are now confusing: 'I am feeling upset because my grandmother died' or 'I failed my exam with severe clinical depression.'

The rise of mental health awareness

It is heart-warming to see how many institutions and charities are getting involved in actions and activities to raise awareness of mental health, mental illnesses and disorders. These are vital to reducing the fear, stigma and discrimination surrounding these topics.

But is awareness on its own enough?

Mental health is being discussed increasingly, but are we talking smart?

I personally believe that we need to go beyond this increased awareness. My conversations with students and HE staff have highlighted that despite the fact that we now have more access to information around mental health and mental disorders, there still seems to be an increased state of confusion. Even though we have now gained more understanding around mental disorders and their treatments, and how to improve and keep our mental health, we still struggle to know when and where to get help and do not appear to have the skills necessary to promote self-care. In our daily lives, we generally take an interest in our physical health but what about our mental health? If I asked you, you would probably be able to say something about a specific 'physical' illness and its symptoms such as cancer, or diabetes but what about 'mental illnesses'? How much do you know about depression, agoraphobia, Obsessive Compulsive Disorder or Post-Traumatic Stress Disorder? What about stigma? Could you explain these naturally and intelligibly?

As Dr Winch (2014) states in his TED talk, it is time that 'we close the gap between our physical and psychological health. It's time we made them more equal.' Einstein said that if we can't explain something clearly, we don't understand it enough. The same applies to mental disorders. It is time to close the gap between our physical and psychological health. It's time to make them more equal.

The way we can do this is by introducing mental-health literacy in education, in our curriculum or our teaching alongside awareness, so that we can all start talking smart about mental health.

The World Health Organization corroborates this idea and states that health literacy is a clear key determinant of health and that 'literacy is a stronger predictor of an individual's health status than income, employment status, education level and racial or ethnic group.' (2013, p.7).

Experts explain that in doing so we pathologize normal stress responses and regard or treat them as psychologically abnormal.

Clinicians and experts in the field define all the above terms very clearly. They also demonstrate that they are not the same thing at all. And so we turn to the wonderful work carried out by Dr Kutcher.

Chapter 2
Time for clarity and understanding – a real need for mental health literacy

'Clarity, clarity, surely clarity is the most beautiful thing in the world'
– George Oppen

The different stages of mental health and why it matters

Dr Stan Kutcher's pyramid model enables us to understand the various mental health states. According to Kutcher et al.'s (2015) book *School mental health: global challenges and opportunities* (pp.302–305), mental disorders can:

> exist concurrently with mental well-being. None of the domains are exclusory to the other domains at one time and a person can be in more than one domain at the same time. For example, a student can have a mental disorder (such as ADHD), be experiencing a mental health problem (such as

the death of a grandparent), be experiencing mental distress (such as an imminent examination); and be in a state of mental equilibrium (such as spending time playing a game with their friends).

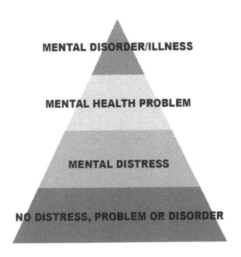

Let's take a closer look at these four mental-health states. I have decided to copy the information *ad verbum* with the author's permission to ensure exactitude and correctness to avoid any confusion:

Mental disorder/illness

Mental Disorder and illness are defined as synonymous and are defined by the International Classification of Diseases (World Health Organization 2014) and the Diagnostic and Statistical Manual (American Psychiatric Association 2013). They will therefore change when these organizations change their definitions.

As it stands here is how both organizations define mental illness or disorder:

'A mental disorder is a clinically significant behavioral or psychological syndrome or pattern that occurs in an individual and that is associated with present distress or disability or with a significantly increased risk of suffering death, pain, disability, or an important loss of freedom.' (*DSM-5*)	• 'There are many different mental disorders with different presentations. They are generally characterized by a combination of abnormal thoughts, perceptions, emotions, behaviour and relationships with others. Mental disorders include: depression, bipolar affective disorder, schizophrenia and other psychoses, dementia, intellectual disabilities and developmental disorders including autism.' (WHO)

Mental health problems

These are emotional, cognitive and behavioural difficulties experienced by an individual arising from a substantive environmental stressor (such as the loss of a loved one, loss of employment, migration, poverty, etc.). While there are substantial differences in how individuals experience and deal with such substantial stressors, all individuals will be impacted to some degree. Frequently, these stressors will result in significant emotional, cognitive, physical, perceptual or behavioural symptoms and even some short-term decrease in usual functioning, signifying difficulties in adaptation that are commonly addressed by community resources and community traditions (such as religious rituals regarding death, self-help organizations) or by socially sanctioned healers who may or may not be medical professionals (such as counsellors, pastoral care workers, etc.).

Mental health problems are not *mental disorders*, and vice versa. Unfortunately, some jurisdictions confuse the two, and use data from mental disorders to define mental-health problems. Such conceptual confusion can lead to medicalization of normal human experience (for example, treating with medications) and conversely, denial of needed treatment for a mental disorder by labelling the difficulties being experienced as a problem and thus not requiring mental health care. Depending on the social situation or geographic context, many individuals in a given population may experience a mental-health problem during the school-aged years (up to age 25).

As indicated at the beginning of this book – as academic tutors we clearly are not trained nor equipped to deal with mental-health problems or mental disorders and should always refer students to ensure that they get access to the treatment they need.

Mental distress

Mental distress is the common, ubiquitous and normal experience of negative emotions, physical, cognitive and behavioural symptoms that occur every day, arising from environmental challenges (for example, failing to get a job; preparing for an examination; experiencing romantic rejection; etc.) and are ameliorated with successful adaptation (leading to learning) and usual social, interpersonal and family support. All students will experience some degree of distress in everyday life. Individuals experiencing mental distress do not require professional interventions and successful overcoming of distress is an essential component of developing resilience. Avoidance of usual distress can lead to incapacity to deal with 'the slings and arrows of outrageous fortune [...] and by [so doing] end them' (Shakespeare 2006).[7] At times, students who are ex-

---

7   Shakespeare, W., in Thompson, A. and Taylor, N. (eds) *Hamlet: the texts of 1603 and 1623*. London: The Arden Shakespeare (2006).

periencing mental distress self-diagnose mental disorder or mental health problems and place themselves higher up on the pyramid.

Mental Equilibrium: No distress, problem or disorder

This is a point in time where the individual (even if they have been experiencing emotional, behavioural, perceptual, cognitive or physical symptoms) is experiencing a positive sense of self, is adapting reasonably well to their environment, and is reasonably content with their state of being, however they define that state of being.

What's the difference between a disorder and a normal stress response?

As we can see from the previous definitions, there is a clear difference between a person experiencing the 'normal stresses in life' and someone suffering from a mental illness or psychopathologies, such as depression and anxiety. The majority of students I interviewed, mentioned 'anxiety' in our conversations. So, let's use this as an example to illustrate the point. There is a difference between the 'normal' anxiety people experience in response to everyday life. Anxiety is part of life in our modern society. I can think of many situations where it is judicious and appropriate to react with some anxiety. For example, being worried about exam failure or about giving an oral presentation is normal. Fear of public speaking is extremely common, not just in the student population. However, there is a distinction between 'normal anxiety' and 'anxiety disorders' which can be more intense (such as panic attacks), will last longer (a feeling that lasts for several months or even longer instead of going away after a stressful situation has come and gone) and which may lead to phobias which then start having an impact on your life. Anxiety can appear in different forms and at different levels.

It may express itself as anything from uneasiness all the way to a panic attack and some variants in between. Students might, for example, develop disproportionate apprehensions about going to school or going out which then turns into a phobia when they avoid the situation and refuse to attend school or university.

Clarification – for whom are the interventions in this book suggested?

At this point in the book, I would like to clarify that the suggested interventions in Parts II and III of this book are intended to be helpful for flourishing and languishing students experiencing no distress or some mental distress, NOT for students experiencing mental illness, disorder or a mental problem. As mentioned in the previous section, there is a clear difference between 'normal' mental distress and mental illness and it is important for tutors to refer the latter to the relevant professionals who are experts in the field of mental health and who know the best solution for such a case. For example, if a student is already having Cognitive Behavioural Therapy (CBT) for something such as anxiety disorder then a tutor without clinical training might embark on work around a student's beliefs about themselves, in a way that might not be helpful, or indeed could be harmful. Similarly, there is a growing body of evidence around the importance of teacher embodiment in the quality of outcomes for those learning Mindfulness, as well as concerns around those with specific vulnerabilities (e.g. clinical depression) engaging in Mindfulness without well-trained teachers who can also offer some level of therapeutic support. Russell and Siegmund (2016) explain that the (mis)perception of Mindfulness as a 'simple technique' belies the complexity and skill needed to deliver a Mindfulness training that has real therapeutic and transformative power. They also propose a framework to help clinicians think through the suitability of Mindfulness for their particular client group with the intention of providing guidance for thoughtful decision-making. It is important to flag up to tutors that it could be especially risky to use the Mindfulness Meditation on emotions proposed in the next section which requires looking at difficult emotions with students experiencing mental disorders or trauma, for example. It might be helpful for you to know at this point that there are specific Mindfulness interventions (such as Mindfulness-Based Cognitive Therapy, MBCT) aimed at such students, which are distinctly different to the light touch suggestions that I have made here in this book.

The exercises in Part II would also be excellent for tutors if they want to develop themselves and to apply these to their own personal experiences because as the coach John Wooden (1997, p.16) said 'the most powerful leadership tool you have is your own personal example'.

What is stress?

After a hard day at work where we constantly answer requests from others via emails or face-to-face, without mentioning some of the issues we have to deal with in the office with our colleagues and at home with our partners, and our children, we often say that we are feeling 'stressed'. It is a sensation that so many students report experiencing on a regular basis.

But what do we mean exactly when we say that we are 'stressed' or 'anxious'?

The impressions and situations that can generate some stress can be different for every individual and for each one of us. When I asked students about this topic they most commonly stated that they were feeling stressed because they felt powerless and that they didn't have the resources to fight against or to master a situation.

Remember: We usually feel stressed because we feel that we are incapable of mastering, dealing or controlling a situation.

Stress affects our body and mind in several ways. First of all, it creates a complex physiological reaction. But what if we considered it for what it is? A natural response of the body also known as the term fight/flight and freeze response from the sympathetic nervous system. This survival mechanism also called hyperarousal or acute stress response was first coined by Walter Bradford Cannon in his two books *Bodily changes in pain, hunger, fear, and rage* (1915) and *Wisdom of the Body* (1932). He described it as a natural physiological reaction that occurs in response to a perceived harmful event, attack or threat to survival. It is the reason why we are still here as a species. It kept our ancestors safe from sabretooth tigers and other predators.

Cannon's theory states that animals react to threats with a general discharge of the sympathetic system as an attempt to prepare the animal for fighting or fleeing. More specifically, in *Bodily changes in pain, hunger, fear, and rage* (1915) Cannon shows how the adrenal medulla produces a hormone cascade which results in the secretion of norepinephrine and epinephrine, which support sensory alertness. The hormones oestrogen, testosterone and cortisol as well as the neurotransmitter dopamine, which supports prediction of reward and motor activity, serotonin which supports autonomic control and emotion and oxytocin which promotes social bonding, affect how we react to stress.

Our brains react quickly to keep us safe by preparing the body for action. Just like animals, humans react to acute stress by either fighting the threat, freezing or fleeing from it. It is a healthy survival mechanism to put our bodies on full alert in case we need to run away, or we suddenly need a lot of strength to save our life. It is there to protect us. Most of the fears that plague us today exist only in our imagination. They are not real threats. But the amygdala cannot tell the difference so the nervous system gets stuck in unnecessary stress responses.

This primitive mechanism is called the 'system of defensive behaviour' (LeDoux 1998). Defence against danger, LeDoux argues, is probably the number one priority of any organism. Furthermore, LeDoux discusses the constant role played by the amygdala in defence against danger across all species possessing an amygdala. He states:

> The remarkable fact is that at the level of behavior, defense against danger is achieved in many different ways in different species, yet the amygdala's role is constant. It is this neural correspondence across species that no doubt allows diverse behaviors to achieve the same evolutionary function in different animals. This functional equivalence and neural correspondence applies to many vertebrate brains, including human brains. When it comes to detecting and responding to danger, the brain just hasn't changed. (p.174)

LeDoux also describes the amygdala as 'the hub in the brain's wheel of fear'.

All primal emotions arise from the amygdala in the limbic brain, the primitive, animal part of the brain. 'A person with PTSD or an anxiety disorder is essentially over-responding to a frightening stimulus,' DeLaRosa et al. (2014, pp.60-61) say. 'The more complete our model of how threat response works in "normal" brains, the better able we'll be to pinpoint what's gone wrong in people who respond abnormally to threats.' Let's take a closer look at how our automatic nervous system works specifically. Getting to know it will enable us to recognize when it is being triggered more effectively.

Key points to remember

This 'flight, flight or freeze' response is there because it prepares us to either fight, run away to escape the danger but if neither of these two options works, and it seems like we are going to be killed by our predator, then we go into a shock state known as the tonic immobility. We do this because we are in a state of fear. Abrams et al. (2009) confirm this when they state that tonic immobility is a temporary state of motor inhibition believed to be a response to situations involving extreme fear, for example during sexual assault or a disaster. This tonic immobility is well documented in animals and we can see it when a cat catches a mouse, which then starts playing dead and does not move.

This flight, flight or freeze response is a fast and automatic 'gearing up' which can prove essential when we are faced with danger. As explained before, this is what enabled our ancestors in more primitive times to survive when we were constantly faced with threatening situations when we either fought a sabretooth tiger or simply ran away from it.

The stress response – what happens in our body

The autonomic nervous system (ANS) is a big network of nerves reaching out from the spinal cord and which affects directly every organ in the body. It comprises two branches: the sympathetic and the parasympathetic, which have completely opposite effects. The sympathetic branch of our autonomic nervous system triggers the stress response and helps us deal with dangerous or life-threatening situations as an attempt at keeping us alive. Adrenalin is released which increases our heartbeat and our blood pressure in order to direct the blood towards numerous muscles so that we can use them to either flight or fight.

Blood is diverted away from the stomach because digestion is not really required in a life or death situation. What is the point of digesting your food if you are going to be someone's dinner?

Functions considered as non-essential in a fight or flight situation are suppressed such as the ability to reproduce, to grow (for children) or to digest.

This also explains why when we are feeling stressed we

report feeling 'butterflies in our stomach' or 'feeling sick'. The blood is diverted from the stomach to the muscles and the brain to provide them with the energy and oxygen they require.

Cortisol is also released to increase glucose in the bloodstream, which also provides more energy for the muscles and the brain. Cortisol improves the brain's ability to absorb glucose and alters the immune system.

As a result of this response, we also experience fear and worries. When we are facing a potential physical danger, these emotions motivate us to pay attention to what is going on around us and to take care of ourselves.

After the danger has passed, the *parasympathetic* ANS takes over, decreasing heartbeat and relaxing blood vessels.

In summary: The flight, flight or freeze response is an automatic reaction which forces our body to shift into high gear. As human beings, we are wired to withstand occasional and extreme stress and our bodies can cope with a lot of pressure. When we lead a healthy life, the two branches of our ANS work in harmony and generate action then rest (and relaxation).

It is possible to experience these effects on our body by imagining a stressful situation. To show you how, I would like you to try a little exercise. Read the instructions below and try to engage with this exercise as much as possible (really notice what you see, hear and feel when you recall the experience).

- Recall a negative event like an argument you had with a friend or with a member of your family. You become angrier and angrier. Again, notice what you see, hear and feel inside. Maybe your heart is beating faster, you are sweating a bit more, your breathing is shallower, your muscles are becoming tense. Not so nice! These sensations come from the sympathetic branch of the nervous system. It is a little bit like the accelerator on the car that revs up to get us into action. The only problem with this is that you may end up crashing, as your brain tells you it is good to rev it up and feel the rage.

Now – look around you and check what time it is. This will enable you to disconnect to the negative feelings and emotions. Now try another exercise for the positive.

- Recall a really positive event like a birthday party or a great time you had with a friend or with a member of your family. It can even be what you would describe as the best day of your life. Again, notice what you see, hear and feel inside. How fast or slowly is your heart beating? What about your muscles - are they tense or relaxed? What about your breathing? I am sure it will be much more enjoyable than the previous experience. These sensations come from the parasympathetic branch of the nervous system. It makes us feel calmer, more relaxed. It does the exact opposite of the sympathetic nervous system.

The thing is that in both cases, the source of stress does not exist as such and is not 'out there'. In fact, it is all 'made up' as it is simply based on a memory of an event. So we get a stress response based on an event that is happening in the moment, based on what we think and on a memory or a combination when certain situations become linked to memories or previous bad experiences.

What does this stress response mean for you as an academic member of staff? Can you think of times when you have experienced this 'flight, fight or freeze' response?

The stress response – an issue in the 21st century?

Our reaction to run away or fight in a dangerous situation was extremely useful for our ancestors who needed to protect themselves against predators. However, nowadays, the situations that generate stress for us are more often linked to psychological threats than physical ones. We don't have to combat or flee even if our bodies are prepared and ready to do so.

It does not matter if the stress you experience comes from someone who is experiencing road rage on their way to work, comes out of their car and threatens you physically or if you are experiencing stress when you read the content of your inbox. The same physical reaction occurs in your body. Each time we perceive something as a threat, it means that you are more than likely to trigger this automatic response.

This reaction is designed for short-term events or situations. The physiological responses which happen during an acute stress period can be extremely useful in the short term but if the stress becomes chronic, it can be really negative for us.

Remember: The fight, flight or freeze response is triggered every time we perceive a threat in our environment. Unfortunately, we cannot change situations and what happens to us in life. What we can change is the way we see them, our perception of events. When something challenging happens in our lives, we need to remember that we are not what happens. What we resist, persists and what we embrace dissolves.

Stress is often presented as a big and powerful external force that is controlling us and that we have to constantly fight. It is often presented as an enemy we need to exterminate but what if it isn't a foe and, in fact, it is a friend that we need to get to know?

Many sportspeople know this and believe that not all stress is bad for them. For example, Rory McIlroy, declared at the 2011 Masters 'you're always going to be nervous teeing it up in a Major Championship. It is very natural and it's a good thing. It means that you want it' (cited in Cohn 2011). Stress can in fact help us feel more alert and more motivated to get up, practise or to get involved with things. It can also help gain a competitive edge. Stress can also help us prepare, focus and perform to reach the perfect level.

Stress only becomes a real danger for our health when it becomes chronic instead of acute. Some of the students who have been diagnosed with a Generalized Anxiety Disorder reported some health-related issues such as sleeping problems, recurring headaches and migraines, aches and pains. In their article, Schneiderman et al. (2005) corroborate this aspect when they indicate that if stressors are too strong and too persistent in individuals who are biologically vulnerable because of age, genetic or constitutional factors, stressors may lead to disease. This is particularly the case if the person has few psychosocial resources and poor coping skills.

Remember: Stress can be good for you. For example, it is what gets me into a room full of people to give a presentation or during an interview and research demonstrates that dealing with short-term stressors or experiencing acute stress typically do not impose a health burden on healthy individuals.

Why stress is good for us

'The truth is that stress doesn't come from our boss, our kids, your spouse, traffic jams, health challenges, or other circumstances. It comes from our thoughts about our circumstances,' states Andrew Bernstein (2010). Although all the symptoms related to stress seem to be very negative, some studies like the one carried out by Kirstin Aschbacher et al. (2013), from the University of California which states that brief episodes of stress may actually be beneficial to our health, protecting us from the effects of aging.[8]

---

8   https://www.researchgate.net/publication/236046079_Good_Stress_Bad_
     Stress_and_Oxidative_Stress_Insights_from_Anticipatory_Cortisol_
     Reactivity

Teitelbaum, author of *Real cause, real cure* (2012) who has studied the effects of stress on immune function, echoes these findings, saying stress in small doses can improve cognitive function and improve our overall health. It would appear that the way we think about stress also has an effect on what happens to us. In her TED Talk,[9] Stanford University psychologist Kelly McGonigal states that throughout her career she has advised her patients to rid stress from their lives because it can have a negative impact on the human body – she has made stress the 'enemy'. However, recent work by Lauren Wisk, PhD,[10] and her colleagues had her revising her approach to stress.

Described in a 2011 American Psychological Association article (Keller et al. 2012), Dr Wisk's team linked survey data on nearly 30,000 US adults to national death records in order to determine the relationship between levels of stress, and the perception that stress impacts on health and health outcomes. They found that both higher levels of reported stress and the perception that stress affects health were independently associated with worse physical and mental health.

Most strikingly, those who reported a lot of stress and that stress greatly impacted on their health together had a 43% increased risk of premature death (over an eight-year period), suggesting that how you think about stress matters just as much as how much stress you have. Thinking that stress is harmful could literally kill us in the long run.

When you change your mind about stress you can change your body's response to stress. McGonigal suggests that when stress is viewed as a positive, something helpful to performance, a person will be able to decrease the negative effects of stress on physical health. McGonigal's suggestion to change our minds may seem easy but as we develop habitual behaviours and thoughts, it may not be as simple and quick to implement.

9   www.ted.com/talks/kelly_mcgonigal_how_to_make_stress_your_friend.html
10 www.ncbi.nlm.nih.gov/pmc/articles/PMC3374921/

The stress vulnerability model

Zubin and Spring (1977, p.110) suggest that:

> ... as long as the stress induced by challenging events stays below the threshold of vulnerability, the individual... remains well within the limits of normality. When the stress exceeds the threshold, the person is likely to develop a psychopathological episode of some sort... when the stress abates and sinks below the vulnerability threshold, the episode ends.

Using the stress vulnerability model enables us to:

- identify examples of stressors and vulnerabilities
- identify some positive coping methods and protective factors
- relate this to the stress vulnerability model and provide an explanation
- use it as an analogy to aid explanation
- create a sketch and a rationale for action.

The stress vulnerability mode has been presented by many theorists but has been presented in the simplest way by Zubin and Spring (1977). The model incorporates identifiable personal vulnerability factors of both a biological (e.g. genetic predisposition, and pre- and perinatal injury) and psychological (e.g. early experiences) kind. Stressful life events that the individual experiences prior to the onset of the psychotic symptoms are then incorporated into the model. This type of formulation has two clear advantages. First, it offers a personalized view of the development of each person's symptoms that integrate the biological, and medical perspective that he or she is likely to have been exposed to. Second, it provides a normalizing rational (Kingdon and Turkington 1991) that points to the idea that everyone has the potential to develop psychotic symptoms if put under sufficient stress. This normalizing of symptom helps to counteract alternative, terrifying models of madness that the patient may hold.

The stress bucket

Practitioners sometimes use the analogy of a bucket of water, whereby the size of the bucket indicates the capacity of the person to cope with stress.[11] This model takes the view that people with schizophrenia are more vulnerable to the stresses and strains of life, such as major life events (losing a job, bereavement etc.) and day-to-day stresses (such as managing bills, or other daily tasks). These can sometimes cumulate to the level where the person's ability to cope is lost, and a relapse can occur.

The 'bucket' analogy describes these stresses as amounts of water being poured into a bucket until the bucket overflows – that is breaking point. It can be very difficult to remove all stresses from someone's life so often the work to be done is about increasing the person's ability to cope – making the bucket bigger!

An analogy of a bucket being filled and overflowing was used to describe the stress vulnerability model. This was put in terms that each person's biological make-up and past experiences shaped how the bucket would be formed, what capacity it had and what weakness it had. Stressful life events and stress factors were described in terms of water filling the bucket and the stress equals the level of water in the bucket. These stress factors may be varied and numerous such as exam pressures, not getting enough sleep, debts, lack of support, relationship issues, death of a close relative. The bucket only has so much room before the water reached the top. Once the volume of water filling the bucket overstretched the capacity, then the water

---

11   See Brabban, A. and Turkington, D. 'The search for meaning' in Morrison, A. (ed.), *A casebook of cognitive therapy for psychosis* (2002).

overflowed – the individual became symptomatic with signs and symptoms such as anxiety, hearing voices and sleep problems. There are vulnerability factors for the individual, which is indicated by the size and strength of the bucket. A more vulnerable person may have a smaller or shallower bucket. Each person may have coping strategies with, for example, holes in the bucket to let out the water and therefore lower the stress levels.

Factors of influence on mental health – biological (genetics) and environmental (epigenetics), cultural and social

According to Weir (2012), some specialists such as Dr Kandel, professor of brain science at Columbia University believe that it's all about biology. Kandel said, 'All mental processes are brain processes, and therefore all disorders of mental functioning are biological diseases. The brain is the organ of the mind. Where else could [mental illness] be if not in the brain?' (cited in Weir 2012, p.32).

Weir (2012) also states that Thomas R. Insel, former director of the National Institute of Mental Health, also championed a biological perspective. To him, mental illnesses are not different from heart disease, diabetes or any other biological components, and he stated that, 'the only difference here is that the organ of interest is the brain instead of the heart or the pancreas. But the same basic principles apply.'

In recent years, scientists have made great discoveries about the function and dysfunction of the brain. Mayberg et al. (2005) have begun to find out physiological explanations for depression. Their clinical study singled out a region of the brain called Brodmann area 25, which is overactive in people with depression. They describe area 25 as a 'junction box' that interacts with other areas of the brain involved in mood, emotion and thinking. They demonstrated that deep brain stimulation of the area can alleviate symptoms in people with treatment-resistant depression.

In *What is mental illness?* (2011), McNally explains 'certain disorders such as schizophrenia, bipolar disorder and autism fit the biological model in a very clear cut sense' (p.185). In these diseases he states, structural and functional abnormalities are evident in imaging scans and during post-mortem dissection. Yet, he also notes that for other conditions, such as depression or anxiety, the biological foundation is more nebulous and that mental illnesses are likely to have multiple causes, including genetic, biological and environmental factors. This is the case for many chronic diseases such as diabetes or heart disease. But for mental illnesses, we are far from understanding the interplay among those factors.

Weir (2012) also explains that complexity is one reason that experts such as Jerome Wakefield, PhD, DSW, a professor of social work and psychiatry at New York University, believe that too much emphasis is being placed on the biology of mental illness at this point in our understanding of the brain. Decades of effort to understand the biology of mental disorders have uncovered clues, but those clues haven't translated into improvements in diagnosis or treatment, he believes. 'We've thrown tens of billions of dollars into trying to identify biomarkers and biological substrates for mental disorders,' Wakefield says. 'The fact is we've gotten very little out of all of that.' (cited in Weir 2012, p.32).

To be sure, Wakefield cited by Weir (p.32) says, some psychological disorders are likely due to brain dysfunction. Others, however, may stem from a chance combination of normal personality traits. 'In the unusual case where normal traits come together in a certain configuration, you may be maladapted to society,' he says. 'Call it a mental disorder if you want, but there's no smoking-gun malfunction in your brain.'

You can think of the brain as a computer, he adds. The brain circuitry is equivalent to the hardware. But we also have the human equivalent of software. 'Namely, we have mental processing of mental representations, meanings, conditioning, a whole level of processing that has to do with these psychological capacities,' he says. Just as software bugs are often the cause of our computer problems, our mental motherboards can be done in by our psychological processing, even when the underlying circuitry is working as designed. 'If we focus only at the brain level, we are likely to miss a lot of what's going on in mental disorders,' he says (cited in Weir 2012, pp.32–33). The danger in placing too much attention on the biological is that important environmental, behavioural and social factors that contribute to mental illness may be overlooked. 'By over-focusing on the biological, we are doing patients a disservice,' Wakefield says (cited in Weir 2012, pp.32–33).

The emerging area of epigenetics, meanwhile, could help provide a link between the biological and other causes of mental illness. Epigenetics research examines the ways in which environmental factors change the way genes express themselves. McNally (2011) stated that 'certain genes are turned on or turned off, expressed or not expressed, depending on environmental inputs.' (pp.159-160) Research suggests that diseases are caused by a combination of different types of changes in many different genes. Some of these changes are genetic mutations that are passed along in families. Some are mutations that happen randomly or because of environmental factors. For example, one of the first classic epigenetics experiments, by Weaver et al. (2004), found that pups of negligent rat mothers were more sensitive to stress in adulthood than pups that had been raised by doting mothers. The differences could be traced to epigenetic markers, chemical tags that attach to strands of DNA and, in the process, turn various genes on and off. Those tags don't just affect individuals during their lifetime, however; like DNA, epigenetic markers can be passed from generation to generation. More recently, McGowan et al. (2009) studied the brains of people who committed suicide, and found those who had been abused in childhood had unique patterns of epigenetic tags in their brains. In McNally's view, there's little danger that mental-health professionals will forget the importance of environmental factors to the development of mental illness. For him, 'What's happening is not a battle between biological and non-biological approaches, but an increasingly nuanced and sophisticated appreciation for the multiple perspectives that can illuminate the etiology of these conditions.' (p.129)

The good news – neuroplasticity – our capacity for change

The Oxford Dictionary defines neuroplasticity as: 'The ability of the brain to form and reorganize synaptic connections, especially in response to learning or experience or following injury.' Our brain is not a complex machine and is not hard-wired and stuck the way it is. It is constantly being changed by experience. You will realize that your behaviours and your thoughts are not the same today as they were ten years ago. These changes are possible because of neuroplasticity, which means that the brain changes its structure and organization through learning, experiences and adaptation.

Our brain is malleable and it means that neuroplasticity is the 'muscle building part' of the brain. So the more you practise a thought or an emotion, the more you reinforce the neural pathway. But if you have a new thought, you create a new neural pathway and a new way of thinking or doing things. Every time you do something and repeat it over and over again, this leads to changes in how your brain works. This new neural pathway will become stronger. The skills you don't use fade away.

Remember – every time you think a thought or act in a certain way, over and over again, it strengthens it. Over time, that way of thinking or that action becomes automatic. You can rewire your beliefs and actions because of what you think or what you do. Neuroplasticity happens throughout life. Connections within the brain are constantly strengthened or weakened, depending on what is being used.

But the good news is that we are not fixed in how we think, learn and perceive and we can change. I would highly recommend watching Sentis's video on neuroplasticity[12] as well as the documentary directed by Mike Sheerin entitled *The brain that changes itself.*[13]

What does it mean for the HE sector?

In the last decade, the concept that all aspects of our life should be happy and stress free has appeared. I am trained in Mindfulness, NLP and Hypnotherapy so I do not disagree with the notion of 'happiness in life', far from it. In fact, I believe that there is a real need for more skills to enhance our well-being: for better relationships, more engagement, more purpose and meaning in our lives (more on this in Part III). The issue with the notion that everything in our life (at school, university, work) should go smoothly and without a 'glitch' is that it conveys the idea that everything we encounter in our daily experience is supposed to be stress free.

This is a huge problem because from the comments made by some students I interviewed, it is possible to see that they don't understand why they are feeling stressed at university, they are not enjoying themselves and they wonder what is wrong with them. When they feel the stress response described earlier in this chapter, they interpret it as a pathology. In some ways, normal life has been pathologized and normal emotions

---

12   www.youtube.com/watch?v=ELpfYCZa87g
13   https://youtu.be/bFCOm1P_cQQ

and cognitions have become pathology and this is clearly a big problem. This leads people to believe that every negative emotion or state they encounter is a trigger for a pathology.

It is important to realize that if we do not teach young people or encourage them to solve problems by using methods which are positives and lead to good outcomes then they are going to turn to negative methods that lead to bad outcomes. This is part of the challenge we are currently facing in our Western societies. In NLP, there is a presupposition which says that 'behind every behaviour, is a positive intention'. This means that every time we do something, it is usually done because we believe it will help us to 'achieve something' or to 'get away from a painful situation'. This is why, for example, young people start self-harming as a way to cope with their intense emotions or students drink a bottle of wine every night. They have found 'an unresourceful state' to cope with their emotions.

If we buy into the notion that normal life is pathology, we start looking for ways to 'no longer be stressed'. But that does not make sense because the stress response which is in every single one of us is the phenomenon that drives adaptation and resilience in life. We wouldn't be here as human beings if we didn't have this faculty, as our ancestors would not have survived.

In their book *The Dangerous Rise of Therapeutic Education*, Ecclestone and Hayes (2009) corroborate this and show how the sorts of activities which were – and mostly still are – prevalent in schools 'embed populist therapeutic assumptions, claims and process throughout education, signifying the idea that emotional well-being, emotional literacy and emotional competence are some of the most important outcomes of the educations system' (p.xi). All of this is predicated on the concept of a 'diminished self': the idea that we are all damaged, vulnerable, emotionally fragile and suffering from low self-esteem. This sends the message that we are somewhat broken individuals who need fixing. They view this as damaging because, 'therapeutic education [is] profoundly anti-educational' and 'whatever good intentions lie behind it, the effect is to abandon the liberating project of education' (p.xiii). In concentrating on what is immediately relevant, inclusive, engaging and reflects students' 'real needs', a 'curriculum of the self' lowers expectation and aspiration, hollowing out and replacing the goals of an academic curriculum. This sense of vulnerability is what has taught learned helplessness to a generation of kids we call the millennial.

In this model, 'learning a body of worthwhile and inspiring knowledge (not simply facts to be repeated), or learning to love particular subjects, or aspiring to excel in them, have become invisible as educational goals.' (p. 62) The therapeutic education does not:

> lift young people out of everyday problems, whether those problems are banal or serious. Instead [it] immerses young people in an introspective, instrumental curriculum of the self, and turns schools into vehicles for the latest political and popular fad to engineer the right sort of citizen. (p. 64)

The issue lies with the current system of testing at GCSE and A level which has recently been introduced in secondary schools. I believe that the current testing format for our students does not help them become better learners. In his article on the implications of learning sciences research, Sawyer (2007) confirms this. He states that by the 20th century, all major industrialized countries converged on essentially the same model of schooling. He also explains (p.2) that knowledge is seen as a collection of facts about the world and procedures for how to solve problems. Facts are information that we may find useful and procedures are step-by-step instructions. The goal of schooling is to get these facts and procedures into the student's head. People are considered to be educated when they possess a large collection of these facts and procedures. Teachers know these facts and procedures, and their job is to transmit them to students. Simpler facts and procedures should be learned first, followed by progressively more complex facts and procedures. The definitions of 'simplicity' and 'complexity' and the proper sequencing of material are determined either by teachers, by textbook authors, or by asking expert adults like mathematicians, scientists or historians – not by studying how children actually learn. The way to determine the success of schooling is to test students to see how many of these facts and procedures they have acquired.

This is especially clear when students arrive at university. Students are bringing with them the legacy of this standard and traditional model of teaching with the constant testing to see if they have acquired the facts and procedures but also the effect of pilots on 'being happy'. Education, I believe, should be about enabling teachers to share their knowledge, passion and enthusiasm for a subject and to empower students to develop their motivation, creativity, curiosity, critical thinking, and enthusiasm so that they discover their own passion for specific subjects and most importantly want to carry on learning throughout their lives.

Yes, some students clearly suffer from mental disorders or experience mental distress and they need access to the right level of help and treatment. Some experts suggest that a mental illness or disorder may be lifelong, but the symptoms may in fact come and go and may not be permanently present in their life. I also believe that, just like any physical illness, it does not have to define who they are and it certainly does not mean that they cannot have mental health alongside their condition and that they cannot lead a normal life.

We all experience difficulties in life. There are some things that provide a challenge and that's a necessary part of being a human being and the way we frame it can enable or disable us.

Take for instance some of the students I interviewed, who were told by their doctors: 'this is going to be a lifelong problem, you can't improve' and yet there are all kinds of evidence that given time they will recover but this notion that somehow you can't live with and recover from certain mental illnesses or disorders is, I think, very disabling.

What clearly stands out is the fact that despite decades of research on the causes and treatments of mental illness, patients are still suffering. Kandel seems to have agreed with this when he declared that, 'We have a good beginning of understanding of the brain' but 'boy, have we got a long way to go.' (cited in Weir 2012, pp.32–33). However, I think that there is hope and that with time we will understand mental illnesses and disorders much better and gain the same understanding that we currently have for other 'physical illnesses' and that we didn't have 100 years ago. Kandel (ibid.) said that 'Schizophrenia is a disease like pneumonia and that seeing it as a brain disorder destigmatizes it immediately.' There is no shame to be had in suffering from a mental illness and perhaps if we described mental illnesses as brain malfunctions it would help minimize the stigma and help people talk about their symptoms more openly and freely, get medical help and treatment in the same way that a cancer patient or heart disease sufferer does.

I even find myself hoping that maybe one day, very soon, we will have made so much medical progress, just as we have with other medical conditions and we will be able to diagnose depression or schizophrenia through a brain scan or a blood test. And it would appear that I am not alone in thinking this way. Leitch, creator of the Social Resilience Model (2015)[14] believes that

> today in part because of the amazing advance in neuroimaging, we can see pictures of how electrical impulses travel in

---

14   www.thresholdglobalworks.com/about/social-resilience/

the brain and what parts of the brain light up when we think, feel or do certain things [...] This can be good news and bad news. The good news is that people can be helped to have greater resiliency by practicing skills that reinforce healthier pathways in the brain. The bad news is that remaining stuck in disabling beliefs, negative emotions and hurtful practices wired dysregulation into the brain.

Would it not be more empowering to use the definition of 'crisis' as 'a time when an important decision must be made' or 'decisive point'?

This 'decisive point' would be to state that the current paradigm leads us to believe that the stress and anxiety experienced by students when they transition from secondary to HE is a mental disorder. This may, however, simply be a helpful alert that things need to develop and change. All this is perhaps due to a lack of skills to bridge the gap between secondary and HE or a clear understanding of what they are experiencing in their own bodies and minds and what is expected of them to achieve good grades as independent researchers and learners.

Several models have been proposed to explain the development and maintenance of depression among youth. Cognitive vulnerability models stand at the forefront of research activity. Beck (1967) defined cognitive vulnerability as the presence of maladaptive self-schema reflecting themes of helplessness and unlovability that become activated by negative life events or negative moods. Many cognitive vulnerability theories employ a vulnerability-stress paradigm (e.g. Abramson et al. 1978; Beck 1967), whereby cognitive factors interact with environmental stressors to increase risk of emotional disorders. Indeed, stressful life experiences predict depression among children and adolescents. Despite advancing understanding, most recent models that place primary emphasis on stress as a key cause of a disorder have difficulty dealing with data showing that even extreme stress is not linked to psychopathology in all individuals (Monroe and Hadjiyannakis 2002); after all, approximately 50% of individuals do not show evidence of a disorder such as depression following significant life stress. Hence, although data convincingly show that stress contributes to depression, they just as convincingly show that other factors also play a critical role.

Important final points to consider

We are not fragile little eggs like Humpty Dumpty, which will fall and break. We are resilient beings, far more than we even know. We have managed to evolve and grow in different environments throughout history. It is important to remind young people of this.

Richardson et al.'s (2012) 'Thriving or just surviving. Exploring student strategies for a smoother transition to University. A Practice Report' based on Australian first-year university students, also confirms this. They compared the experiences of 'thriving' students with those who described themselves as 'just surviving'. One interesting aspect is the 'mental health changes' reported by students. When students were asked to rate changes in their mental health during their first year, some alarming yet not surprising changes were noted. None of the 'thriving' students reported their mental health as changing in a negative way during their first year, either reporting that it had stayed the same (53%) or changed for the better (47%). They also stated that university either met or exceeded their expectations in a positive way. On the other hand, 63% of the 'just surviving' students rated their mental health as changing for the worse and described university as being worse than they had expected. Only one student stated that his mental health had improved and this was regarding the learning of new topics of interest. Feelings of stress, anxiety and being overwhelmed were very common. The ability to cope with stressful times during the year was also explored, and was another area where large differences existed between these two groups of students. Thriving students described using strategies that were much more focused on taking action related to the stressor in order to deal with the stress and then be able to relax afterwards than the 'just surviving' students. Most of the 'just surviving' students nominated passive or avoidance strategies for dealing with the stressful event, which tended to leave them feeling even worse once they were required to return and deal with that stressor.

The next sections of this book will aim at introducing specific tools for students and tutors to take action rather than passive avoidance.

- PART II -

THE IMPLICATIONS FOR EDUCATION

Chapter 3
Time for a new model?

'Education is the most powerful weapon by which you
can change the world'
– Nelson Mandela

Emotional, mental, physical, social, spiritual health – always kept separate

In our Western societies, we are taught to look at our thoughts, emotions, bodies and interactions separate from one another. We seem to keep them completely independent and compartmentalized. But what if they were in fact not separate but intertwined? Could our mental health have an impact on our physical health or our physical health have an impact on our emotional, social and mental health?

What if Thomas Merton (2011) was right when he said that 'If a man is to live, he must be all alive, body, soul, mind, heart, spirit'?

Some specialists also seem to agree with this idea. In her article entitled 'The nervous system and resilience' (2015)[15] Leitch states that the term 'mental health' is outmoded. She adds 'We know that the mind and body are a system, inseparably connected; so we really need a term that reflects interventions that explicitly work with both.' (p.1) Pert (1999) described this as 'body-mind'. Others use 'holistic' or 'integrative' models. The fact that there is not a term that is universally used and understood reflects the fact that this is a relatively new frontier for psychotherapists and other clinicians and practitioners. This also links with the research on the gut microbiota, which has become a focus of research particularly for those interested in the brain and behaviour. For example, according to Dinan and Cryan (2015) the gut microbiota has recently been profiled in a variety of conditions including autism, major depression and Parkinson's disease.

What if they are all a 'continuum'? Corey Keyes's model as an exemplar

Prior to the progress made by modern medicine, we would consider someone to be physically healthy if they were not stricken by an illness. Nowadays, all the progress and technology has changed our definition of physical health. It ranges from total fitness to being unfit (due to several aspects such as no physical activity, nutrient and diet, drugs, cigarettes and alcohol consumption, self-care for example looking after oneself when we suffer from a cold, rest and sleep). But when we are physically unfit, it doesn't mean that we suffer from an illness. Of course, the longer we carry on our unhealthy habits, the more likely it is that we will develop an illness such as high cholesterol, cancer or diabetes.

---

15 www.thresholdglobalworks.com/pdfs/nervous-system-and-resilience.
    pdf

What if the same applied to emotional, mental, physical, social and spiritual health?

The mental health continuum: from languishing to flourishing in life

As we have previously seen, mental health is a 'state of well-being'. Keyes (2002) describes it as a 'syndrome of symptoms of positive feelings and positive functioning in life' (p.46). He reviewed and conceived of dimensions and scales of subjective well-being as mental-health symptoms. A diagnosis of the presence of mental-health is described as flourishing, and the absence of mental health is characterized as languishing.

When reflecting on Keyes' concept, we realize that it is possible to have either a high mental health (or flourishing) and a low mental health (or languishing). We can go up and down the continuum depending on various factors but this does not mean that we are suffering from a mental illness or disorder. In fact, it is actually possible to be diagnosed with a high mental illness or disorder but to be flourishing at the same time and to be able, as WHO (2004) states, to 'realize our own potential, cope with the normal stresses of life, work productively and fruitfully, and be able to make a contribution to our community'. (p.1) The stories shared by the students certainly support this idea.

It is also possible to be languishing and have a mental illness or to be flourishing with a low mental illness or no mental illness and finally to be languishing with a low or no mental illness.

HIGH MENTAL HEALTH
(Flourishing)

Flourishing &
Mental Ilness

Flourishing

Moderate
Mental Health &
Mental Illness

Moderate
Mental
Health

**HIGH
MENTAL
ILLNESS**

Languishing &
Mental Illness

Languishing

**LOW
MENTAL
ILLNESS**

LOW MENTAL HEALTH
(Languishing)

According to Keyes, mental health is more than the presence and absence of emotional states. Emotional well-being is a cluster of symptoms reflecting the presence or absence of positive feelings about life. Symptoms of emotional well-being are ascertained from individuals' responses to structured scales measuring the presence of positive affect (e.g. individual is in good spirits), the absence of negative affect (e.g. individual is not hopeless) and perceived satisfaction with life.

People with mental disorders want to be accepted and to be accepting of others and themselves, to contribute and belong, to express their ideas and opinions. They are not different from anyone else. Keyes argues that his idea can be applied literally to everybody regardless of whether you are suffering with a mental disorder. For him, our illness is simply a small part of what constitutes us and what we must deal with in order to face this task of trying to flourish.

What is a flourishing student versus a languishing individual?

In his chapter, 'Complete mental health: An agenda for the 21st century', Keyes (2003) defines languishing as a state where the individual is devoid of positive emotion towards life, is not functioning well psychologically or socially and has not been depressed in the past year.

He also states that complete mental health includes three clusters (emotional, psychological and social well-being) and provides us with a clear definition for the qualities a flourishing individual would have (p.299).

Positive feelings: emotional well-being which includes:

Positive affect: the person is regularly cheerful, in good spirits, happy, calm and peaceful, satisfied and full of life.

Happiness: the individual feels happiness towards past or about present life overall or in domains of life.

Life satisfaction: sense of contentment or satisfaction with past or present life overall.

Positive functioning: psychological well-being and social well-being:

Self-acceptance: positive attitude towards oneself and past life, and concedes and accepts varied aspects of self.

Personal growth: insight into one's potential, sense of development and open to challenging new experiences.

Purpose in life: has goals, beliefs that affirm sense of direction in life and feels life has purpose and meaning.

Environmental mastery: has capability to manage complex environment and can choose or create suitable environs.

Autonomy: comfortable with self-direction, has internal standards, resists unsavoury social pressures.

Positive relations with others: has warm, satisfying, trusting relationships and is capable of empathy and intimacy.

Social acceptance: positive attitude towards others with acknowledging and accepting people's complexity.

Social actualization: cares and believes that, collectively, people have potential and society can evolve positively.

Social contribution: feels that one's life is useful to society and that one's contributions are valued by others.

Social coherence: has interest in society, feels it's intelligible, somewhat logical, predictable and meaningful.

Social integration: feels part of, and a sense of belonging to, a community, derives comfort and support from community.

WHO's definition of health and link with the new concept of 'flourishing student'

If mental health does not simply equate to a lack of mental illness but equates to a whole state on its own, 'a state of well-being' or 'flourishing'– how would you react to this sentence: 'there is a state of well-being or flourishing crisis' among students? How about 'a state of well-being problem or issue'?

You would probably think that as a French native speaker, my knowledge of English is not very accurate or fluent and yet, we all to some extent seem to use the same collocations with the word 'mental health' without even questioning it.

Therefore, I would argue that it would be far more beneficial to ask why some students struggle to accomplish this state of well-being which would enable them to realize their own potential and cope with the normal stresses of life, work productively and fruitfully and most importantly contribute to their community.

So, is it time to review this paradigm, this set of linguistic items that form mutually exclusive choices and to find a new word which could be used by all? Shall we simply apply the WHO's definition more freely and frequently in order to bring more positivity?

Is it time to focus on well-being and health based on a balance between emotional, mental, physical, spiritual and social health and not as separate entities?

The positive dimension of mental health is stressed in WHO's definition of health as contained in its constitution: 'Health is a state of complete physical, mental and social well-being and not merely the absence of disease or infirmity.' (2005 No 2, p.100)

Finding a balance between positive and negative may not be as easy and straightforward as it seems and may not be a straight 50-50 split. As part of his research on healthy relationships, Dr Gottman (1998) discovered that relationships were functional, happy and stable, if and only if the ratio of positive to negative interaction during conflict was greater than or equal to 5:1.

In 1969 Boucher and Osgood published a paper entitled 'The Pollyanna hypothesis' in the *Journal of Verbal Learning and Verbal Behavior* in which they concluded that 'humans tend to look on (and talk about) the bright side of life.' (p.1) Jing-Schmidt (2007) argues that we create and use more good words not, as Bierwisch (1967), suggests because of people's tendency to consider the good as the normal state of life and the bad as the abnormal but in the hope that we can verbally construct a safer world for ourselves precisely because the good cannot be taken for granted in the real world.

I cannot help but wonder if using this 'Pollyanna hypothesis' or the 'positive bias' instead of the 'negative bias' in the current language use around 'mental health' would help us construct a 'safer world' for ourselves and our students. If so, what positive words might we want to use? 'State of well-being' and/or 'flourishing'?

Chapter 4
A new model based on students' stories

*'You never change things by fighting the existing reality.
To change something, build a new model that makes the
existing model obsolete'*
– R. Buckminster Fuller

Some of the students I interviewed reported that when they arrived at university they regularly felt lost and lonely. This is quite normal, as they have lost their connections and left their support network back home. Imagine. They used to go to a secondary school where they were told that they were A* star students, that they were amazing and that they could do and achieve anything they wanted. Their teachers really supported them and helped them organize their workload and plan their essays by looking at their plans, drafts and by making regular suggestions. Teachers also designed lessons around them and their preferences. They lived at home and their parents did a lot for them and then suddenly, they arrive in a new city, they are put in halls of residence and asked to make new friends and to get on with their academic work at university, which is so different from what they are used to. This could be described as the 'big fish in a small pond' syndrome. Students report that they are experiencing not only social but also cultural isolation, which leads to a real culture shock. We normally associate culture shock with experiences in a foreign country or abroad but Oberg's (1960) early definition was: 'Culture shock is precipitated by the anxiety that results from losing all our familiar signs and symbols of social intercourse.' (p.177) P. Adler's (1975) definition of culture shock is psychologically more descriptive and explanatory:

> Culture shock is primarily a set of emotional reactions to the loss of perceptual reinforcements from one's own culture, to new cultural stimuli which have little or no meaning, and to the misunderstanding of new and diverse experiences. It may encompass feelings of helplessness, irritability, and fears of being cheated, contaminated, injured or disregarded. (p.13)

N. Adler's (1981) definition highlights the chaotic and fatiguing nature of culture shock when she defines the construct as, '... the frustration and confusion that result from being bombarded by unpredictable cues' (p.343).

Another commonality was the fact that many of the students suddenly experienced what they described as 'life difficulties' and for some of them it was the first time they did, as things always 'went smoothly before then'. One student described it by saying:

> My dad had an affair in my second year – a few family members close to me died in my first and second year. When I got back from my year abroad my boyfriend of 3 years split up with me. I had planned to move in with him and I had to move in with random people. My drink got spiked and I ended up in hospital at the beginning of my final year.

Most of them wish that they had asked for help immediately at university rather than letting it build up. They also wish they had tried finding coping mechanisms and discovered what worked best for them. We could compare this ability to identify new sources of support in a new environment with the ability that a plant's or flower's roots must react to its environment. In the article, 'The intelligent plant'[16] (2013) Pollan explains that scientists have found that the tips of plant roots, in addition to sensing gravity, moisture, light, pressure and hardness, can also sense volume, nitrogen, phosphorus, salt, various toxins, microbes and chemical signals from neighbouring plants. Roots about to encounter an impenetrable obstacle or a toxic substance change course before they make contact with it. Roots can tell whether nearby roots are self or other and, if other, kin or stranger. Normally, plants compete for root space with strangers, but, when researchers put four closely related Great Lakes searocket plants (*Cakile edentula*) in the same pot, the plants restrained their usual competitive behaviours and shared resources.

So, where do we start?

The flourishing student model

As I researched for this book and came across the flourishing concept, it immediately made me think of a flower and I have decided to use the notion of flower as an analogy to represent the student and their experience when they arrive at university. This is when the *Flourishing Flower Model* came to life.

This metaphor of the flower suggests that it is a continuum and an ever-changing state that fluctuates for the flower, each of its petals, moment to moment, day by day. The flower will open or close depending on how each of its components is doing.

---

16   www.newyorker.com/magazine/2013/12/23/the-intelligent-plant   [accessed 11/12/16].

If you look in nature and observe flowers, you will see that to be in full bloom, a flower needs to be totally open with all its petals wide. You will also notice that all flowers are different. In spring, rows and rows of daffodils appear on the side of the road and some are taller, smaller, yellower, whiter, more orange than others. They don't seem to look around asking themselves and others 'why am I taller than you?' or 'why are you bigger/yellower than me?' They simply are. They are firmly rooted in the soil, simply being themselves in the present moment, in the now. This is the notion I would like to encourage with this metaphor.

Everybody is a flower or a flowering plant. We are all different types of flower. We can be daffodils, sunflowers, ivy or water lilies. This means that we will have completely different needs and we will all look different too. This is true of us as individuals. We are all unique individuals with different strengths, weaknesses and with different interests and passions. This is particularly useful to remember in the context of education as students always tend to compare themselves to others and to see how well or badly they do in comparison to others. If the student accepts the fact that he or she may be a sunflower and that one of their peers might be a bluebell, they would not feel the need to compare themselves to others and would simply accept to be the flower they are. They would understand that it is in fact pointless to compare themselves to others.

But we all have one thing in common: as mentioned at the end of Part I, we are not fragile we are all resilient and we can take care of our own needs and have real abilities for growth and to thrive. One example to prove this is the fact that as we grow up we slowly learn to speak or to crawl and walk and even when we fall and hurt ourselves, we still get up and continue and try over and over again. We don't simply 'give up' because this 'walking malarkey' is far too difficult.

It is then also possible to accept that if you are an ivy you are likely to be far more resilient and able to climb walls than if you are a sunflower or a poppy. If as a member of staff (acting as a member of the gardening team or caring for the flower), I treat you (the sunflower) in the same way as I treat the ivy and expect the same thing from you then it isn't going to work. I cannot expect you to climb up a wall, as you are more likely to spread than to climb. That's what you do best. So as a tutor, I am one of the gardeners in this university garden (I am one of the many people in this gardening team who are involved in tending to the students' needs, including other university staff but also friends, family and others outside the university environment). I will look at what you do best and I will try and encourage you to grow as well as possible by providing you with all that you need as a sunflower.

Of course, this game of comparing ourselves started at a young age so it is not going to be easy to introduce change but it is entirely possible, particularly if we accept this notion both for ourselves and encourage our students to do the same. In fact, I think it starts from the minute we start using language because we are taught what things are and what they mean. We then start comparing different objects with each other. Our parents, without even realizing, compare us to our siblings and that's when this game is introduced in our life and becomes habitual.

From my conversations with students, it is obvious that when they were in secondary school, as flowers, students felt that they were surrounded by other flowers which were much more like them; many of them also felt that they were in a safe environment that provided them with all the nutrients, water, light, etc. they needed. In fact, they were safe in their home garden too, surrounded by their friends and family. They had a real support network.

Going to university meant that they were uprooted from their 'comfortable patch' and put into a completely different soil. Based on what students said, it would also seem that when they arrive at university these flowers are set into a specific soil which might not be best suited to them. This would therefore mean that we cannot plant all the flowers in the same soil and simply expect them to 'get on with it' in this new environment.

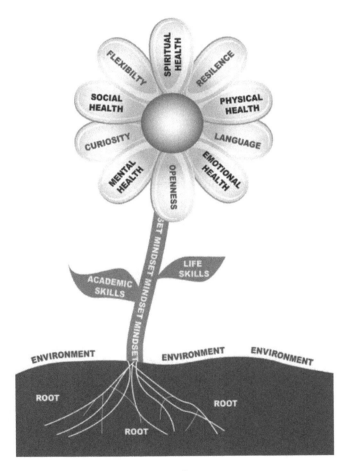

The university as a garden

I particularly like the metaphor of the university as a garden. The idea would be to encourage every Higher Education Institution to recognize that it is like a garden that contains a huge variety of plants and flowers which will require different care to flourish. These flowers are all unique and individual but put together they create a great composition that makes up the overall garden with different colours, shapes and scents.

The environment

In the same way that a flower's growth is dependent on many factors such as the amount of light, water and nutrients so does our 'flourishing flower model'. The way our 'student flower' grows will depend on the environment, our gardening skills but also how well it absorbs the nutrients it is given. With proper care, the flower can grow and flourish in the soil that contains the right mixture.

If you look at the diagram you will see that it is not simply the flower but also the environment. The idea is to represent the 'system' and not simply an individual (as the flower) and 'the environment' as two different entities that have no impact on each other.

In many press articles, there is often a cause and effect way of presenting the issues experienced by students at university: 'Going to university stresses students out', but as this image shows, it is not as simple as that. The setting or environment has an impact on the flower but the flower also influences the system. All the people who are part of a HEI system are not only part of the problem but also part of the solution. We all impact on the system and it is important that we all become aware of this.

The soil is therefore the environment – the way the flower opens or closes is codependent with the environment and it might 'flourish' much more in one environment than another. The blossoming of the flower will also depend on how rich the soil is. As tutors, we form part of this environment and I will discuss this interaction further in Part III. We can help our stu-

dents flourish by providing them with the right 'nutrient' and
'food' they require. It may also depend on our 'gardening skills'
and the care we provide our students. Students may for example respond to our own feelings of stress and anxiety.

We need to look at the model of the flower with the student
being the full flower. We as academics need to see our students
and their experience as a whole and not as fragmented. This
means that we need to look at the environment and how we
contribute to making this soil as rich and fertile as possible. For
a plant to grow, it needs sun, water, nutrients and a good soil.
So, with this metaphor – how is the soil in Higher Education
helping students to flourish? We need to make sure we realize
that whilst we see our interactions with students as unique, students see their experience at university as whole and each person is part of the bigger picture. We are all interconnected and
we impact on each other's experience. We need to take responsibility for our interaction with students and realize that they
are different than their peers were ten years ago. The new generation has needs that are different and we need to take them
into account. One of the students I interviewed said that she
felt that tutors at the university were the only adults she could
talk to and share with when she arrived but that sometimes she
felt some tutors were not open and didn't really want to have
a discussion with them. She also mentioned that she wouldn't
want to discuss some of her personal issues with some tutors
because they wouldn't understand or relate to her experience. I
think it is extremely important for us as tutors to ask questions
and to make sure that students feel welcome and that they become integrated within the university.

Although the environment has an impact on the flower
and how well it is flourishing, it is also important to ensure that
students understand that they are not simply dependent on the
care they receive from the members of staff and academic tutors. They are also responsible for taking in the nutrients and

taking care of themselves. A good gardener can give the plant all the nutrients and water it needs, it will not flourish or look beautiful if it doesn't absorb any of it and transmit across all its relevant parts. This is also true for our 'student flower'. They are responsible for the absorption of the information provided by tutors, for example.

When I use the word 'responsible', I refer to the concept of 'response ability', the ability to choose your response (as introduced by Jack Canfield 2006) to external events. We are not victims of external events and we can decide how we respond to an event that happens in our life.

As Senge explains in *The fifth discipline* (1990), it is also vital that students become aware of the 'enemy is out there' syndrome or what he describes as the 'propensity in each of us to find someone or something outside ourselves to blame when things go wrong." (p.8).

When things are difficult it is so easy to look at the external event to believe that it is happening TO us rather than FOR us. Blaming others and things may initially make us feel better but in the long term it is vital to get out of the victim mentality and mode of functioning and to accept that as an individual we are responsible for the way we stand in the soil – how we take on the nutrients, the water, the sun that is being provided to us. We would not blame the sun when we are in the shade, for example, we would simply move. Students can take responsibility. Isn't it powerful to know that we can choose our reaction to an external event? I often say to my two boys that their names are not Pinocchio and that they don't have strings that people can pull to make them feel or do anything. They always can choose and have a choice. They can choose their response to what is happening in their lives.

Why does this matter? In Higher Education, so often I hear young people who say that because they are paying a lot of money for their education, they are entitled to more things, more help and more support. And whilst it is true that they deserve the best education possible and that they are entitled to attend classes that they love, that will help them become the successful graduate but most importantly the successful human being they want to become in their chosen field I believe there is an issue around what universities are actually designed for. Is it to prepare students for life or to solely impart knowledge? Do we try to develop the whole student or just part? If we look at students holistically, we as academic tutors need to ensure that their environment, their soil, is as nutritive and empowering as possible so that they can grow and flourish. But it is also each individual student's responsibility to take on the nutrients, and the water and to absorb them if they want to grow and flourish. We cannot do this for them.

This is the same if you go and have private sessions at the gym with a trainer. He or she can show you how to do the exercises and what food you need to eat to improve your level of fitness and to lose weight but he or she cannot do the push-ups for you nor can he do the healthy eating or the endurance training. This is also true of our relationship with students.

The idea here is not to induce guilt, which is a very unresourceful state. We always do the best we can with the resources we have. So, there is no point in blaming oneself and feeling bad. The reality is that the most empowering step to take is to accept that regardless of what is currently happening in our life, we are ultimately the one who decides to hang on to a feeling or thought or to do something about it.

Flourishing students seem to take responsibility for the way they feel and think. They seem to know what they need more than anybody else because they are aware that they live with themselves 24/7. Nobody else does. They appear to do the best they can with the resources they have when things happen.

It can be that as a flourishing student they realize that they can do better in different 'environments'. For example, a student might not flourish as well in their halls of residence at the beginning of Year 1 as they do in their school or department or when they go back home because these are all different settings. The important point is to be aware of this and to notice how as an individual flower they stand in the various environments and how they respond to them.

As I have mentioned before, we are not wooden puppets with strings that people on the outside can pull to make us feel or experience. Yet, we tend to use language and vocabulary that suggest as such when we say: 'he made me sad' or 'he upset me'. I know it is not easy to accept at first and of course, I am not saying that some people's behaviour can't be irritating or frustrating but I firmly believe that people can't make us feel or experience anything. We can choose our response and this is where our 'response ability' lies!

The roots

As mentioned before, the flower is firmly established in the soil through its roots. These are strong and hidden from view. They include past experiences and memories, the values and beliefs, the metaprograms or strategies we use to make decisions, the hereditary traits inherited from our ancestors.

Memories

These are all the individual and collective experiences that have an impact on our current perceptions. Our present behaviours are significantly influenced by our collections of memories. For example, if you burn yourself on a stove, you will remember not to touch it the next time.

Values

These are the things that are most important to us. Values are our next most unconscious filter and are based upon our experiences to date. Values are linked to our beliefs and influence what we consider to be right or wrong, good or bad. Values are context specific, therefore what is important in one area of your life, may not be important in other areas.

Beliefs

These are what support our values. Beliefs are what we hold to be true, about ourselves, others and the world. They are thoughts that we have thought consistently over a long period. Whether religious or not, we all have beliefs, and the quality of our beliefs significantly influences the quality of our life.

The metaprograms

This is a Neuro Linguistic Programming (NLP) concept that enables us to get to the way we process information. They are extremely important, as they will give us an indication of how people process information and data. If we pay attention to the language used by students (not just the content) but the words, it is possible to discover some metaprogram preferences and how they can impact on the way we deal with situations. There are seven main metaprograms.

1. 'Big picture' or 'small picture': Do you need details before you can start seeing the big picture or do you actually need a vision or a big picture before you can work on the details of a plan?
2. Towards or away from: This is all about your motivation. Do you tend to be motivated more by the end goal (towards) or by the idea of moving away from something negative (away from)? Again, if you are 'away from', I will need to use relevant language to motivate and energize you which will differ from the vocabulary used by a 'towards' person.
3. Options or procedure: Do you prefer clear instructions

and procedures so that you know what you are doing or do you prefer options and really enjoy when things are flexible and can be changed or when you can improvise?

4. Internal or external: Do you make decisions based on your own internal criteria or yardstick or do you need external feedback and information to help you decide that you are doing the right thing or before making a decision?

5. Proactive or reactive: Do you tend to start something and get going straight away or do you wait until people start and then follow?

6. Match or mismatch: Do you tend to notice similarities first or do you notice differences? Do you prefer noticing when things are the same or how different things are?

7. Self or others: Do you tend to view things from the self and based on 'you' or do you see things from the point of view of others? If you want to influence a student who is focused on the 'self' it will be important to focus on the personal benefits they will gain.

It is important to remember that these metaprograms are not negative or positive, they just are and we use them in an 'unconscious way' hence why they are hidden in the roots. They will show in our language (part of the petal) if we listen carefully, and in the language of others. Please also remember that they may change depending on the environment and that they are a blend so may be different when you are with your family, friends, boss, playing a competitive game, etc. Being curious and paying attention to our metaprograms as well as students' is extremely useful as we can use language that is more likely to influence and have an impact on the student and their experience at university.

Specific tools for the teacher:

Exercise 1 – Identify your values

A quick exercise to recognize and identify your values in life and what matters the most to you.

Let's see what is important to you in life; what your values are. They guide our every decision and the satisfaction or violation of them can produce strong emotional reactions.

Now have a go:

The simplest way to discover your values is to ask yourself the following questions:

What is important to you about [topic]?
What do you want in/out of [topic]?
What would having [topic] do for you?

So, for example – what is important to you in life?

Answer: honesty, authenticity, integrity, connections, love, kindness.

Can you then rank them by order of priority or preference? Very often we fail to notice that when people do or say things we don't like it is because they are 'trampling all over' (as I call it) our values. Once we recognize this, it is easier to deal with the person or the situation and to recognize that whilst this is important to us, our values might not be shared or seen as extremely important by others. We learn to accept that it is not good or bad. It just is the way each human being values aspects of life.

You could ask a more general question about 'life' in general or you could focus on other areas like 'relationships', 'family', 'work', 'business' etc. You can decide all the parameters yourself.

_____

_____

_____

_____

_____

_____

Exercise 2 – Identify your beliefs

A quick exercise to recognize and identify your beliefs and to see if they are empowering or limiting you.

Now have a go:

Think about some of the beliefs you hold about various topics (including yourself) and note them down below. Decide and classify them as limiting or empowering. For each belief that you have identified, decide if they are limiting or empowering. If they are limiting, what would be a better more empowering belief?

e.g. I believe that I can meet and connect with new people easily and effortlessly (empowering belief) or I struggle to make new friends (limiting belief).

Start by asking yourself the following question: What do I believe about [topic]? Answer: I believe I am… [fill the gap]

In Exercise 3, I will show you how to change these beliefs with a simple belief change exercise.

Belief	Limiting/Empowering
Example: I struggle to make new friends	Limiting

To download and access the PDF for these two exercises, please visit www.flourishingstudent.com and register.

Exercise 3 – Simple belief change

A belief is only a thought that we keep thinking and it can easily be changed by changing the way we think about something. If you don't believe me think back about when you were a child and you believed in the tooth fairy or Father Christmas. When you discovered that it was in fact your parents, you changed the way you thought about both and created a new belief – they don't exist. This is the same with any belief you may have. For example – I can't do this easily.

John Seymour shared this powerful exercise with us on our NLP practitioner course.[17] I have used it since then and I hope you find it as powerful as I have.

Now have a go:

1. Identify limiting belief and check that students are 100% happy to change it. If there is some incongruence, identify what is worrying them and turn it into a positive.
2. State current belief in the present tense and write it down.
3. State in 'used to believe' tense.
   Get the student to imagine the old belief behind them in the distant past.
4. What would be more useful to believe instead?

---

17   www.jsnlp.co.uk/

Invite student to think of two or three options and then get them to choose the best option for them.

5. Imagine this new belief is now completely true.
   What will be the best thing about this new belief as it becomes increasingly true? Ask student to imagine the new belief becoming true and how different they would feel.
6. Could this new belief cause any problems?
7. What will be the first thing you see, hear and feel as this starts to become true?

Belief	I 'used' to statement	Two or three options	What would be more useful to believe instead?	Imagine the new belief as completely true
Example: Change takes time	I used to believe that change takes time	I can take a small manageable step every day Change can happen quickly Change is easy and quick		

To download the PDF worksheets for these exercises visit www.flourishingstudent.com and register.

The stem

The stem of the flower feeds from those roots and it represents the 'mindset' – the set of attitudes we hold. For the stem to be strong – we need to have strong mindsets.

For example, whether we believe we can grow or if our tutor or teachers expect us to grow, how we define failure and success, understand and receive feedback (Dr Dweck's (2007) growth mindset/fixed mindset). This will have an impact on our academic skills and our life skills, which grow from the stem and are being fed by the mindset or stem.

But the new generation of students and learners also need to take responsibility for their own flower and their own whole experience. This means looking at their stem – the mindsets - and being willing to embrace change and being committed and engaged with the environment they find themselves in. It might mean having to learn new academic and life skills that they do not yet possess and most importantly to embrace the five skills – language, resilience, flexibility, openness and curiosity – and looking after their five 'healths', which we will discuss later on.

One of them is based on the 'growth mindset' as opposed to the 'fixed mindset', which was discovered and highlighted by Carol Dweck. She explained that when students are told that they are clever, or intelligent when they do an exercise, they are less likely to want to take on a new challenge than if they are told that they did a 'good job' or made 'a great effort' when they tried to perform a task. For students to be flourishing, they need to embrace the notion that they have a 'growth mindset', which means that their identity as a learner is not 'fixed' or 'set'. In the past they have been told that they are A* students and that they are bright and clever but several of the students I interviewed told me they felt that they were not clever, how they believed they didn't deserve to be at the university because they realized when they arrived in class that they were surrounded by other A* students who were as good as them, if not better. Suddenly they were with others who were better than them and they were not so sure about their identity any more. The beauty of having a growth mindset is that we first recognize that we don't have an identity – we ARE NOT an A* star student but we have skills, knowledge and understanding or not. It does not mean that if we don't, we cannot acquire it, far from it. It just shows us that there are things we need to learn and we can start asking questions freely because we are not afraid about what others may think or not about us.

The same goes with the notion of failure – at least three students I interviewed explained how afraid they were of failing and this notion that failure was almost like annihilation. But what if failure did not exist? Thomas Edison who created the light bulb said that he found 100 ways of not making a light bulb. There is also a Japanese saying that goes like 'success is falling down seven times and getting up eight'. This means that every time we do not achieve something, we get feedback instead and it tells us where we stand and where we are in comparison to what we want to achieve and we can see how we can bridge the gap.

For example, if one of our tutees comes to see us with their first mark and they tell us that they are not happy, we can start by explaining this concept of 'there is no failure, only feedback, no errors/mistakes only learning'. So many first-year students arrive at university and are used to the concept of As and A*s and they really struggle with the marking system in Higher Education – this concept of a first, a 2:1., 2:2 and so on.

The important thing for their toolbox is to understand what is expected of them – do they understand the question of the essay or what is asked of them for their assignment, that they have looked at the marking criteria and that they understand how they are going to be marked and assessed – what specific parts of their essays will be assessed – structure, content, for example – and that they are clear as to what makes a difference between a first and 2:1 and they then try to structure their essay to meet these requirements.

Reassuring students to show them that the mark does not tell them how clever or able they are but that it simply reflects how well they performed in their assignments and how well they responded to the question asked. A 58 or 62 is not a failure. It simply provides the student with feedback and tells them where they are on the scale and what they need to do next time to bridge the gap between where they are and where they want to be – maybe move to a low first or a high first. When we give feedback to our students, it is important that we ensure we provide them with that 'feedforward' as tutors so that if they haven't yet clearly understood that the mark is not a reflection on their level of intelligence but a reflection on their ability to use their critical and analytical skills to analyse a specific topic or subject.

The interesting thing is I can relate to this concept and that no doubt so can you, to some extent. In our lives, we all have dreaded receiving feedback from people because we see it as a reflection on us, on how good or not good we are at what we do. During the interviews for this book, a couple of students stated that they avoid reading feedback because they 'take it personally, their sense of achievement is bound up with a sense of self and they start to believe that it shows that they are not good enough to be studying at university'.

This leads nicely on to the third topic in mindset, which is feedback – students often see feedback as criticism of things they 'did wrong'. But feedback on an essay gives students further information on the parts which were good and on what they did very well in their work, the parts which need improving and how they can do this – by for example learning to quote others better or by using secondary literature to 'back up' their arguments. Feedback is not used to back up the notion of 'intelligence and identity as a good student or good learner' but simply to show students where they can improve what they did on a piece of work or topic. Encouraging students to engage with feedback is therefore vital if students want to grow, develop and improve.

I highly recommend using the sandwich feedback with a change in the language going from good, better to best – so the first bit of bread is all about the good parts of the essay, what the student did well and achieved in their work, the better part gives the student the 'meaty' bit they always expect with the word 'but' but this time as a tutor, we provide our students with all the important aspects of the work they need to focus on to improve (or 'feedforward') and we finish with the best part of the essay or coursework. What we love the most about it.

Specific tools for the teacher:

Exercise 1

Ask them their definition of failure and success. Ask yourself how you would define failure and success. Is it the same? Different?

If working in groups, spend some time discussing these similarities and differences and decide on a common definition of 'failure' and 'success' that everyone is satisfied with.

Exercise 2

Ask them to define what 'growth mindset' and 'fixed mindset' are. Discuss these definitions and decide on a final definition students can remember and use on a daily basis.

Exercise 3

How do they receive feedback?

Ask your students how they view feedback? Very often students see feedback as a form of criticism or as a way of pointing out what they have done badly or incorrectly. Flourishing students seem to engage with feedback as they see it as a way of understanding what they can do differently next time and what they can improve. As with exercises 1 and 2, encourage open discussion and conversations around the fear that receiving feedback generates for students. It is also an opportunity to discuss the fact that the mark is not the 'be all and end all' and that in fact feedback is what will enable them to gain a better grade next time.

For me feedback is a little bit like a sat nav. It's the little dot that locates you on the map and tells you where you stand on the scales (from first class piece of work to third class) and tells you how to bridge the gap between where you currently find yourself and where you want to go. It's nothing to be afraid of and it enables us to change, improve and grow so should always be welcomed and accepted. Even if I do admit that sometimes it is not easy to get feedback, particularly if it is presented in a 'harsh' way.

Questions: How do you define feedback? How do you feel when you receive feedback? What do you do when you get an assignment back? Do you tend to look at the feedback or simply the mark? Why?

Exercise 4

Get them to challenge their beliefs around these concepts (you could use the previous exercises on identifying beliefs about feedback) and ask them what their reaction would be to this sentence:

There are no mistakes only learning – no failure only feedback

When my boys started primary school (each in turn) and went to reception, I bought them each a nice pencil and a rubber and I then told them that it was their best friend and they shouldn't be afraid of them for every time they use the rubber to erase a mistake, they have learned something. They are now in Years 2 and 4 respectively and I can confirm that they are not afraid of making mistakes. What would happen if we gave students a rubber and a pencil when they start university and if we introduced these concepts to make sure that the 'stem' of their flower is strong and can lead to the acquisition of new academic and life skills they will need as part of their new environment?

Life and academic skills

Life skills and academic skills are closely linked and impact on the results students get at university greatly.

'If you don't know where you are going, you might wind up someplace else' – Yogi Berra

Academic skills

Academic skills involve action planning, goal setting and chunking down to take back control. When the amount of work they have been set, the essays they have to write, overwhelms a student I often suggest that they use the 'chunking down' technique.

Chunking down means to look at a task and to cut it into smaller parts that can be subdivided and clarified to help with the workload.

Action planning

This is an activity which can help students to concentrate on their different ideas and to decide what steps they need to take to achieve specific goals they have. It is presented in a one-line sentence or statement that clearly defines what they want to get done over a specific length of time. It enables students to achieve their objectives in life and to start planning for their future rather than being worried about it.

It requires the identification of objectives, prioritizing the various activities linked to the objectives and defining the various steps required to reach goals. Students can use lists in order for example to meet a deadline or to cope with the pressure of juggling various tasks.

Of course, this is not new for students as this is a task that children learn to do from primary school and in particular in secondary school when their teachers ask them to note the Learning Objective or the WALT (we are learning to…) for each lesson. The idea is to encourage students to do this by themselves, independently and spontaneously so that they can identify what they have learned or achieved either in a week or every day for example.

Identifying key issues and key outcomes

Issues can be defined as what we find problematic in our lives. These issues may involve people, emotions, money, work, tasks, family.

I believe that issues can be very positive and can help us grow. We can learn a lot from the issues we encounter in life and can develop new skills or create new outcomes.

Positive psychology corroborates this with the concept of post-traumatic growth (PTG). Haidt (2006 p.135) cites Nietzsche's quote 'What doesn't kill you makes you stronger.' He also addresses the notion that stress and trauma can be good for people.

Haidt also states that PTG is a direct contrast to post-traumatic stress disorder where individuals find no benefit from their trauma only pain and anxiety.

Previously psychology tended to see stress and anxiety as negative and causing problems but recent research on traumatic events ranging from divorce to death and natural disasters or terrorist attacks (Haidt 2006) shows that even though the causes of post-traumatic growth are vast, the benefits reported fall into three main categories.

- The individual feels stronger and finds hidden abilities and strengths. It changes the person's self-concept and gives them the confidence to face their challenges. For example, the positive belief that things happen not to us but FOR us and to serve our further development.
- The individual strengthens their relationship.
- The individual changes their priorities and philosophies concerning the present and the now and others (Haidt 2006 and Shaw et al. 2005).

When I interviewed students who had experienced traumatic or difficult events, those who felt that they had recovered from the situation clearly reported that they thought they had grown emotionally, developed closer relationships with family and friends when they started discussing their issues and sharing with them and looking at life from a different perspective and considering issues as 'less important'.

It is therefore important to be able to identify what some of our issues are in life. Initially, it is probably best to start with the smaller ones but as students build competence at dealing with their issues, they can start exploring more important ones. It is important to start slowly and to be gentle on oneself but also to have both issues and outcomes in our life plan.

The ability to set outcomes is something we need to learn as it is not innate. Defining outcomes will enable students to define what works best for them.

It is important to be aware of the beliefs and thoughts held about setting outcomes. If students feel that it is going to be hard work and difficult, then chances are that it will be. As Henry Ford said 'whether you think you can or you can't – you're right'. Seeing outcomes as a skill that can help them achieve more will be very beneficial for students.

From the main outcomes we set, we can draw daily outcomes that will enable us to take the steps which will lead us to successful completion of the outcomes we set.

It is a good idea to encourage students to set daily outcomes through journalling, as it will give them a sense of taking back control and being back in charge of their lives. When practised daily, this will become a habit and it will make a big difference to the way they organize their daily activities and plan for the future.

Specific tools for the teacher:

Well-formed issues and well-formed outcomes

This activity will help you and students to identify key issues and set key outcomes. This is a skill that I learned when I trained with John Seymour and that we can develop and learn through regular practice so that it becomes a daily and unconscious habit for success. Identifying key outcomes enables us to gain the best benefits in each area of our life we have chosen and identified. We identify two or three options and we can then pick the best.

Now have a go:

Identifying the well-formed issue or problem:

Sometimes we are much better at expressing what we don't want to happen or to get than what we would rather have. A well-formed issue is likely to involve emotions.

Start with the following question:

What problem or issue are you currently experiencing? Just state in the negative:

e.g. I don't want to fail my exam because I will feel awful and not good enough

To identify the well-formed outcome ask yourself or your student: what would you rather have instead?

State in the positive: I want to pass my exam and feel good.

Check you really want this – If I could pass my exam and feel good – would I take it? Would I be happy with that?

If yes, then continue. If no, then ask what is worrying you about this?

e.g. I am not sure I can do this. Changed statement. I want to believe I can pass my exam and feel good.

Specific information: If I had a magic wand and could give you this right now, describe what would be happening?

Followed by: What would you be seeing, hearing and feeling?

Finally, ask if this is within your control – is this something you can achieve yourself? You can only control your own behaviours. You cannot influence others' decisions, thoughts or attitudes so it is important to focus on what YOU can achieve.

If you don't have an issue to solve, you can then focus on what you would like to do over the next couple of months. You can do this by asking yourself the following question:

What do I wish to achieve next?

I want to…

(state the sentence in the positive) and then follow the steps for the well-formed outcome described above.

To download the PDF for this exercise visit www.flourishingstudent.com and register.

Life skills

The World Health Organization (2003) defined life skills as 'abilities for adaptive and positive behaviour that enable individuals to deal effectively with the demands and challenges of everyday life'(p.1).

Life skills prepare a student to live in an independent way within a society.

Life skills and academic skills provide students with three main outcomes: effective learning, effective living and employability. It involves setting well-formed outcomes or goals and, using their summarizing and memorizing skills, students develop an understanding of the challenges required to adapt to student life, manage personal stress effectively, conflicts and relationships with family and friends, and most importantly to problem solve.

Life skills include specific skills such as:

Job-related skills – writing a CV, time management, presentation skills, planning skills, teamwork.

Everyday living skills – shopping, cooking, washing, managing one's finances which are vital parts of independent living; problem solving, the ability to ask for help when required.

Self-reflection and understanding, stress management, critical thinking.

Some of these skills may not be as developed in young people and this is certainly something I noticed when I rejoined the university after a nine-year break. What young people could do in 2005, their peers do not seem able to do as effectively today. Of course, it is important not to generalize and to say that this is the case for all students but there is clearly a lesser ability to deal effectively with the demands and challenges of everyday life. As we saw in Part I, these could be explained as consequences of 'overparenting' or 'helicopter parenting' and of the fact that many schools are guiding students through their GCSEs and A levels step by step. It would be interesting to research this further to see how these factors impact on students and their flourishing abilities.

The head of the flower

The 'head' of our flower is composed of five 'health concepts' – emotional health, mental health, physical health, spiritual health, social health and five 'skills' – flexibility, openness, curiosity, resilience and language use.

Before we start looking at each 'health concept', let's address the importance of moving through life on 'autopilot'.

Life on 'autopilot'

The Urban Dictionary defines autopilot as: 'when you do something without realizing what you're doing (usually results in making a mistake)'.

In 1983, experimental psychologist George Mandler used driving an automobile as an example in his 'Presidential address to Division 1 (General Psychology) of the American Psychological Association'. He described how a person first learning to drive must concentrate on the workings of various controls, paying full attention to every action. This is the *learning* phase. Later, after much experience, driving becomes familiar and no longer requires full attention. An experienced driver can 'drive on autopilot', letting the mind wander. Driving on autopilot is a fine example of *automaticity*.

Using the same analogy of driving on 'autopilot', have you ever driven on a motorway, deep in thought, only to realize how far you'd gone? Have you ever closed your front door without thinking only to go back to double check because you can't remember doing it? Or have you ever walked back home from university but forgotten to stop at the shop when you wanted to?

This is what I mean by life on 'autopilot'. We are not conscious or aware of our thinking, of what we do on a daily basis. For example, we leave our keys and phone somewhere without focusing on the location and we then spend five or ten minutes looking for them in a frenzy.

People sometimes fail to notice salient unexpected objects when their attention is otherwise occupied; researchers such as Kreitz et al. (2015) describe this as inattentional blindness.

I would suggest watching this great video entitled 'The Monkey Business Illusion'[18] by Daniel J. Simons, which really illustrates this point.

A break from autopilot

A recent study, entitled 'A wandering mind is an unhappy mind' (2010), completed by two psychologists: Matthew A. Killingsworth and Daniel Gilbert from Harvard University, can be found in the journal *Science*. Through their research, the authors concluded that people spend 46.9% of their waking hours thinking about something other than what they are currently doing, and this mind-wandering makes them unhappy. In fact, in their work, Killingsworth and Gilbert argue that 'The ability to think about what is not happening is a cognitive achievement that comes at an emotional cost.'[19]

In a recent article entitled 'The danger of going on autopilot',[20] Dr Ira Hyman (2014) explains how he published a research project on being on autopilot with his former students Ben Sarb and Breanne Wise-Swanson ('Failure to see money on a tree').[21] They placed obstacles on some of their campus walking paths and observed people move past those objects. For example, they placed a signboard on a path (announcing

---

18 www.youtube.com/watch?v=IGQmdoK_ZfY&feature=youtu.be

19 http://science.sciencemag.org/content/330/6006/932

20 www.psychologytoday.com/blog/mental-mishaps/201404/the-dangers-going-autopilot

21 http://journal.frontiersin.org/Journal/10.3389/fpsyg.2014.00356/abstract

that a psychology research project was happening). The sign-board was placed such that people had to move to avoid it. The good news is that no one walked into the sign, not even those on a mobile phone. When asked a few moments later if they had passed any obstacles, some people were unaware that they had avoided a signboard. People using their mobile phones were particularly unaware. Dr Hyman states that this looks like being on autopilot – people avoiding an object but having no awareness of it. Their minds were somewhere else while they moved through the environment, without running into things. For him, they were autopilot zombies stumbling through the world without awareness.

But one really important question according to Dr Hyman concerns just how good our autopilot is. Clearly my autopilot can help me walk across campus while thinking about something other than the walk. Your autopilot sometimes gets you home walking while your thoughts are somewhere else. But are you safe in those situations? Is your autopilot a good driver? Not really. Dr Hyman, his colleagues and other researchers have found that people on mobile phones are slower to respond to a variety of signals in the environment – in their study, they moved later to avoid the signboard, for example. In driving simulators, when people's minds wander, their driving changes. When driving or walking, it's important to be aware of what the objects around you are. Cars, trucks, bikes and pedestrians all move differently and you need to respond differently to avoid them. Your autopilot may not be smart enough to respond well. In addition, much of navigating involves planning – but your autopilot doesn't plan. That's the job of conscious awareness. This is probably why you forget to stop at the store on the way home: consciousness is in charge of planning and your autopilot just follows the road and makes last-second adjustments to avoid obstacles.

Learning to become more conscious of our thoughts, emotions and sensations and directing our attention to them may also make us more aware of the arousal of the sympathetic or parasympathetic nervous system.

Leitch (2015) believes that understanding key reasons for the way we feel, think and act as we do can decrease the tendency to pathologize symptoms as character flaws or weakness. According to her, this sensation-level self-awareness is the key to living an embodied life, being grounded in the present moment, and being able to restore nervous system regulation using the SRM skills.

Emotional health

The Mental Health Foundation has described emotional health as 'a positive state of wellbeing that enables the individual to be able to function in society and meet the demands of everyday life' (Kadam and Kotate 2016).

Emotional health is also the degree to which students feel emotionally secure and relaxed in everyday life. Do they know what a flourishing emotional health looks like, feels like?

Our emotions act as our guide. They lead us to making decisions and taking actions or not. Students I interviewed referred to their emotions as their 'gut feeling' or 'sensations' they experienced and which sometimes might motivate or deter them from doing something.

From a young age, we are taught to control our emotions. For example, as a child if we are sad or hungry, or annoyed and we start crying, our parents tell us to stop. I believe emotions are meant to be felt and experienced. As Peter McWilliams (1994) stated, 'emotion is energy in motion'. It is meant to be experienced and then it disappears. Young children are again great examples of this as they might have a massive tantrum, roll themselves on the floor and then get up and start playing again.

As human beings, we need to start being with our emotions a lot more and to accept them. Very often, instead of acknowledging how they are feeling, students interviewed stated that they saw their emotions as embarrassing, wrong or something to be ashamed of. They often reported telling themselves that they 'are silly to feel this way' and that they often try to ignore the emotions, brush them under the carpet or push them away. I really like the analogy of a pressure cooker. If we keep pushing things down and down, at some point the pressure kept inside the pressure cooker will have to come out and usually it explodes because we haven't used the 'release valve' to let some of the pressure out.

When we are emotionally healthy, we tend to feel relaxed, our body is relaxed and not tensed, we are open to new experiences and new ideas. We have less automatic reactions as well as less anxiety and panic over events in our lives. It also means that we are likely to be calmer and more patient with ourselves and others.

As a result, we also do not judge or criticize our emotions, we accept them for what they are and if we react to a situation, we do not judge or criticize ourselves or others. We recognize as we have mentioned previously that we always do the best we can with the resources we have at the time and high hindsight is fantastic but we didn't know how to deal with an event prior to this, otherwise we would have reacted differently. There is therefore no point to feel guilty about it all.

Several of the students I interviewed reported not feeling safe and secure in their own emotions and feelings and said that they tried to avoid or control their emotions most of the time. They also mentioned at times they felt that their interpersonal and public interactions with other individuals were affected by their own feelings and emotions. This in turn affected how 'open' or 'closed' they felt towards the person.

They also stated that they would like to learn to express their feelings in healthy, assertive ways and not to inhibit their emotions.

They also admitted that there was a clear difference between a negative versus a positive attitude to life but that at times there was a certain feeling of lack of control that led them to procrastinate and to make ineffective decisions for their work and their personal lives.

One skill that seems to help students become more aware of their emotions and of their feelings is the practice of Mindfulness.

Specific tools for the teacher:

Mindfulness to become more aware and present

What is Mindfulness?

The Oxford Dictionary defines it as:

> A mental state achieved by focusing one's awareness on the present moment, while calmly acknowledging and accepting one's feelings, thoughts, and bodily sensations, used as a therapeutic technique.

Over the last 40 years, a lot of studies have been taking place to research and analyse the benefits of Mindfulness. Gunaratana (2002) explains that Mindfulness meditation has its roots in Zen and Buddhist meditation; for example he tells us that Vipassana, a form of meditation that derives from Theravada Buddhism, is a Pali word for insight or clear awareness and it is a practice designed to gradually develop Mindfulness or awareness. A secular practice was introduced by an American Doctor, Jon Kabat-Zinn through his Mindfulness-Based Stress Reduction (MBSR) programme, which he launched at the University of Massachusetts Medical School in 1979.

Kabat-Zinn is considered as one of the founders of the Mindfulness research movement. For this reason, his definition of Mindfulness as 'paying attention in a particular way: on purpose, in the present moment, and nonjudgmentally' (1994, p.8) is one of the most recognized definitions of Mindfulness in the world.

It is particularly important and useful to see Mindfulness not simply as a tool but as a way of life. This means that we stay focused in the present moment, in our bodies, with our emotions, able to observe our thoughts and to spot some recurring thoughts. Mindfulness also involves connecting to others, and practising compassion and loving kindness, which are so important for our social health.

I do not believe that being human requires us to be like monks and to constantly meditate. I also think that too much introspection can also be dangerous as it can make us focus too much on what is going on 'inside' and 'within' and to become slightly self-centred. We are social animals and as we will see later on with 'social health', it is important for us to also turn to the world and to communicate with people if we want to flourish.

It is simply a question of using these great skills and to turn Mindfulness into something we do on daily basis. We are present. We do not rush to the future constantly worrying about what is going to happen next and we do not revisit the past, feeling sad and nostalgic, sometimes wishing that we could change things we have done or said or change what people did or said to us.

It is all a question of balance. My intent with this book is to provide you with information about mental health but also help you gain direct awareness to what you are paying attention to, your language, behaviours, likes/dislikes/preferences and how you make sense of the world and give it personal meanings. I strongly believe that ideas are not set in stone and are context- and stress-related and so can be changed. This is true for all of us. The best way to do so is by gaining said awareness because once you become aware, it opens a spectrum of possibilities which change your view of the world. It's not 'this or that', 'stereotyping' or 'pigeonholing'. Instead it is accepting a spectrum and a range of possibilities and to feel at ease with this idea.

This awareness allows you to gauge, evaluate and calibrate in different situations and with different ideas, and people. As a result, you regain control, which is something students often reported as lacking during our conversations.

Developing a clear understanding of Mindfulness

When I trained in Mindfulness with MindSpace,[22] Adam Dacey taught me all that I am about to share with you. I learned how many others and I lead very busy lives. When I train people in Mindfulness, be it students or staff, they often declare: 'I would practice Mindfulness if I had time but I am really busy', 'I have a lot to do'. We get up early in the morning, have a very quick breakfast. We rush out of the door to rush to work. During lunchtime, we eat a sandwich whilst checking emails or getting on with some work. When we come home in the evening when everything is done, we try to relax in front of a film or by surfing the net or by cracking open a bottle of wine (or all three at once).

Days, weeks, months and years go by like this, living on 'autopilot'. We know that we are alive but we are not aware of the present moment.

On autopilot, we don't realize that our mind is so busy. Buddhists call it the 'monkey mind' because it goes from one thought to the next like monkeys jump from one branch to the next. Restless! We fully associate with the thoughts, the feelings and the emotions and don't even notice it!

---

22 www.mindspace.org.uk/

What Mindfulness really means is being aware of our emotions, feelings, physical sensations and our environment, moment by moment. It gives us an opportunity to really experience life as it is. We become the observers of our lives. We take a step back and observe what is going on in our mind.

It also requires acceptance. This means that we need to pay attention to our thoughts and feeling without judging them as 'good' or 'bad'. Through Mindfulness we learn to tune in to what we are experiencing in the present moment rather than revisiting the past or imagining the future.

Mindfulness is in fact a series of meditations and we will choose something in particular as the object of our focus and attention.

When we are training in Mindfulness, for example by learning to be mindful of sounds, we may notice that our mind becomes distracted by our thoughts, emotions, bodily sensations. This is completely normal when you first start.

To remember that we are supposed to be focusing on sounds and returning our attention back to it is Mindfulness.

The practice of sitting and training in this way helps us to train in Mindfulness. It helps strengthen our ability to focus and through neuroplasticity, we can see how new parts of the brain develop.

If we can practise regularly, ideally every day, we will be able to 'rewire' our brain and we will start seeing the benefits in our lives.

The four ingredients of Mindfulness

When you learn to become mindful, you will also notice that you:

- *Let go of your monkey mind and mental chatter*

As mentioned before, through Mindfulness it is easier to become increasingly able to observe thoughts and feelings. As a result, it will be easier for you to notice and therefore to distance yourself from the constant mental chatter and thinking. You will become aware of the surprising amount of thoughts you have daily and how many come and go throughout the day. You will improve your ability to decide whether you want to engage with these thoughts, emotions, feelings and sensations as opposed to being a victim and simply following them and engaging with them, making up stories and totally identifying with them.

- *Learn to live in the moment*

Lao Tzu (2009) said 'if you are depressed, you are living in the past. If you are anxious, you are living in the future. If you are at peace, you are living in the present.' (p.49)

If you stop and think about it, it makes sense. We have all experienced these anxious or depressed feelings whilst thinking about what happened to us or when we miss something or someone or when we anticipate or worry about something that might happen in the future. All you have that is guaranteed is this moment RIGHT NOW, reading this book or listening to the sounds around you, inside and outside the room you find yourself in, maybe you can hear a clock ticking? The now. This moment is the only thing guaranteed. The rest, the past is gone forever and the future is yet to come… Why worry about it? Some people feel that it is not exciting enough to stay in the present and they enjoy the drama of discussing what might happen or what happened but if you really stop and try, you will notice that the present holds a mysterious feeling which is so strong and makes you feel so peaceful that any 'drama' will pale in comparison and will seem worthless.

- *Give up judgement*

As Jon Kabat-Zinn (1994, p.8) states paying attention non-judgementally means that we stop having strong opinions ('this is good', 'this is bad') about what happens in our lives but rather accept that things are the way they are. There is no point in fighting against what is because it will not make it change. It is useful to learn to be alert and to stay with whatever is happening in the present moment. We often get angry, annoyed, frustrated very quickly almost on autopilot. Mindfulness gives us the ability to respond to things as they are and to accept things as they are. The reality is that we cannot change things most of the time. Because as Heraclitus said, 'Change is the only constant.' As human beings, we seem to spend so much time trying to change what we don't like or complaining about what is because we do not like it. All this energy spent like this is fruitless. It would be so much better to learn from nature and to be more like animals and plants who simply are and enjoy the situation. In autumn, a leaf does not cling on to the branch because it does not want to fall. When it is ready to fall it does so and the beauty is that this leaf will serve the tree because as it falls on the floor and starts decomposing, it will become compost for the same tree it was attached to not so long ago.

- *Develop detachment*

As you learn to practise non-judgement, you will also discover that it is easier to become detached from old views and perceptions. When you become the observer of your life and of the present moment, you will discover that some ways of thinking are not useful anymore and you will be more able to let them go.

The benefits of having a regular Mindfulness practice

Over the last few years, there have been many studies that have empirically demonstrated and supported the advantages of Mindfulness. Whilst Siegel (2007b) highlights that activities such as yoga, t'ai chi and qigong are all practices and disciplines which encourage the cultivation of Mindfulness, the focus on this book will be on Mindfulness Meditation as described by Walsh and Shapiro (2006, p.228) as a family of self-regulation practices that focus on training attention and awareness in order to bring mental processes under greater voluntary control and thereby foster general mental well-being and development and/ or specific capacities such as calm, clarity and concentration.

Shapiro and Carlson (2009) have suggested that Mindfulness Meditation can also serve as a means of self-care to help combat burnout rates.

With more research, there is an increasing body of evidence-based affective, interpersonal and intrapersonal benefits of Mindfulness such as:

- *Emotion regulation*

The research carried out by Farb et al. (2007) and Williams (2010) suggest that Mindfulness meditation shifts individuals' ability to employ emotion, regulate strategies that enable them to experience emotion selectively, and that the emotions they experience may be processed differently in the brain.

Emotion regulation has such strong empirical support as a benefit of Mindfulness meditation that recently the term 'mindful emotion regulation' was coined to refer to 'the capacity to remain mindfully aware at all times, irrespective of the apparent valence or magnitude of any emotion that is experienced' (Chambers et al. 2009, p.569).

- *Decreased emotional reactivity and increased response flexibility*

Findings in several studies carried out by Ortner et al. (2007) suggest that Mindfulness meditation practice may help individuals disengage from emotionally upsetting stimuli, enabling attention to be focused on the cognitive task at hand. They also support the notion that Mindfulness meditation decreases emotional reactivity.

Mindfulness enables us to become more mindful of our everyday activities, more present. In the moment. Most of our time is spent either in the future or the past, which leads to anxiety because of the gap between the NOW and where our mind is. We are missing a lot of our life. Mindfulness brings us in the present moment. It is important to remember that whilst it is important to spend some time observing our thoughts, emotions and feelings and to do some introspection, the purpose of life is to be lived and experienced. As human beings, our primary focus is to live our experiences and our lives fully, exchange with others, love and be loved.

It makes you notice your thoughts, feelings and emotions and makes you realize that YOU are SEPARATE from them. They are just that: a thought, a feeling or an emotion

You are always one thought away from changing your life, if you so desire!

- *It helps relieve stress and anxiety as you become the observer of your life and untangle yourself from thoughts, feelings and emotions.*

By training in Mindfulness Mediation, it is possible to learn and develop the ability to detach from our thoughts, feelings and emotions and to be peaceful and calm instead. Participants in my courses report being able to notice the habits they have created around their thoughts and feelings and feel much more empowered to change them.

A recent meta-analysis of 39 studies supports the efficacy of Mindfulness-based therapy for reducing anxiety and depression symptoms (Hoffman et al. 2010) and a study of Chinese college students by Tang et al. (2007) strengthens the above ideas by indicating that those students who were randomly assigned to participate in a Mindfulness meditation intervention had lower depression and anxiety, as well as less fatigue, anger and stress-related cortisol compared to a control group.

- *It allows you to become aware of people around us and develop greater empathy and compassion.*

Part of the sitting practice helps us to become less focused on ourselves. We can forget our own worries and issues. As a result, we are naturally more focused on what other people are saying. We become better listeners as we are in the present moment. We can hear what people are saying instead of waiting to say our piece. This will definitely improve our relationships.

For example, Wang (2007) used a passive design and found that therapists who were experienced Mindfulness meditators scored higher on measures of self-reported empathy than therapists who did not meditate.

In addition to empathy, another characteristic that seems to derive from meditation is compassion. Kingsbury (2009) investigated the role of self-compassion in relation to Mindfulness. Two components of Mindfulness, non-judging and non-reacting, were strongly correlated with self-compassion, and two dimensions of empathy, taking on others' perspectives (i.e. perspective taking) and reacting to others' affective experiences with discomfort. Self-compassion fully mediated the relationship between perspective taking and Mindfulness.

Mindfulness and the meditation on sounds

This meditation focuses us on the sounds around us – in and outside the room we are in. We simply concentrate on what we hear – we become aware, notice and let go until another sound reaches our ears. We do not make up stories or engage with any of the sounds but use them as the central point of our attention. If a sensation, an emotion or a bodily sensation diverts our attention, we simply notice, acknowledge, let go and bring our attention back to the sounds. We do this over and over again. That's the practice.

Now have a go:

The ideal situation would be for you to find a comfortable place where you will not be disturbed and listen to the MP3.

To download the MP3 for this meditation – visit www. flourishingstudent.com and register.

If you cannot download the MP3 simply follow these simple steps:

Ensure that you have your feet flat on the floor or if you are doing this lying down that your back is straight, shoulders gently relaxed. Gently close your eyes. If you don't feel comfortable closing your eyes, just focus your gaze about one metre away from you – a gentle gaze. Listen to the sounds around you. The focus – you are focused on what you can hear around you. We are not making up stories about these sounds. We simply notice, acknowledge and welcome them and then let them go and move to the following sound we can hear. If your mind has gone off on a tangent or you are being distracted by a thought, a sensation in your body or an emotion, simply become aware, notice, acknowledge the object of distraction and bring your attention back to the sounds. You do this over and over again. That's the practice. I would recommend starting with a three- or five-minute meditation. If you are doing this by yourself, you can use a timer.

Exercise 1 - Mindfulness and meditation on emotions – emotions as our friends

This meditation focuses on our emotions. We bring back a memory that generates emotions (they don't have to be too strong), which we would normally label as 'good' or 'bad'. We then imagine taking them out of our body and observing them. Do they have a colour, a shape? Do they move? Are they cold or hot? We befriend our emotions and notice where they sit in our body so that next time we experience a similar sensation, we will remember that it is our friend.

Once you have finished, write down how you are feeling. Are there any changes in the way you feel before and after? How do you find Mindful Listening AND Mindful Emotions? Reflect on what you learned today. Do you have a preference? Remember, it is YOUR practice and your strategies so be curious and look for what works best for you.

Now have a go:

Read the following instructions and then try this exercise for yourself:

Find a comfortable position with your feet flat on the floor. Gently close your eyes and take a nice deep breath. And again. For a minute or so focus on the sounds around you (same exercise as mindful awareness). Now, bring a memory of something that you would use to describe being 'happy', it can be an event that makes you really smile or a person. It can even be the best day of your life so far. Notice what you see, feel and hear as you recall the situation and identify where you feel this emotion in your body.

Once you have a strong connection with the emotion, imagine that you can take this emotion out of your body. Look at it. Does it have a shape? A colour? Movement? Is it hot or cold? This is your specific representation of 'happiness'. It is specific to you as a unique individual as others might not represent it in the same way as you do. Get acquainted with it and become friends with it.

You can then do the same thing with other emotions such as 'anger', 'sadness', 'pride', 'stress' etc.

The beauty of this exercise is that it shows you that you don't have to be experiencing an event to feel the emotions. Memories trigger the same sensations. The more we befriend our emotions and get to know them, the more we become comfortable with them as and when they arise in our bodies.

You can download the MP3 by visiting our website.

Exercise 2

Ask students to draw their own emotion(s) based on exercise 1.

Exercise 3

Ask students: what would you say to your best friend about this situation?

Write down what you believe that people you love or your best friend would say to describe you and your qualities.

Exercise 4

Ask students: what can you control? What can't you? How can I enhance my control in these areas? It is empowering for students.

Mental health

Our mental health is linked to our logic, our thinking, our understanding. Without our mental health, we cannot survive. Thanks to our thinking, there is some continuity in our thinking and we can understand the world around us; others. We often fail to see how important the thoughts we think are to our success or failure and to what happens in our life. As mentioned before, because we are often on autopilot, we fail to observe our thoughts and our mental chatter and we simply identify with the situation and the thought without challenging them and taking them for what they are – something that can be changed. The problem with thoughts is that if we keep thinking the same thing repeatedly, they become a belief. When we identify fully with a situation and believe it totally, it becomes difficult and almost impossible to change whereas if we are aware and notice that it is our thinking that creates our views of a situation, we can adopt the notion that change is possible. David Bohm, quantum physicist, summarized this beautifully when he said 'thought creates reality and then says I didn't do it' (1994, p.27).

Braden (2012) confirmed this when he stated:

> In the instant of our first breath, we are infused with the single greatest force in the universe—the power (of thought) to translate the possibilities of our minds into the reality of our world [...] an awesome power and our knowing that we are never more than a thought away from our greatest love, deepest healing, and most profound miracles. (p. 17)

Corcoran et al. (2010) explain that Mindfulness meditation promotes metacognitive awareness, decreases rumination via disengagement from perseverative cognitive activities, and enhances attentional capacities through gains in working memory; these cognitive gains, in turn, contribute to effective emotion regulation strategies.

Evidence provided by Siegel (2007a) indicates that Mindfulness meditators develop the skill of self-observation that neurologically disengages automatic pathways created from prior learning and enables present moment input to be integrated in a new way.

Observing our thoughts is like taking a step aside and becoming an observer, a fly on the wall, and we can then see ourselves thinking. We do not try to run away from the flow of thoughts or to even stop them because this is virtually impossible. What happens is that we become aware of the thinking but we don't engage or listen to it.

In Zen, they use the metaphor of the waterfall. We are between the waterfall (the flow of our thoughts) and the rocks (our bodies). We shift slightly to observe our thinking. We are not under the flow of water (we have enough distance not to get caught up in them) but we are not far either (we have enough presence to be aware).

We use our ability to reflect and to self-observe and we simply learn to watch our thoughts go by without trying to suppress them, as it will create the opposite. We don't go looking specifically for our thoughts but simply acknowledge or accept each one as it comes up and let it go.

Moore and Malinowski (2009) compared a group of experienced Mindfulness meditators with a control group who had no meditation experience on measures assessing their ability to focus attention and suppress distracting information. The meditation group had significantly better performance on all measures of attention and had higher self-reported Mindfulness. Mindfulness meditation practice and self-reported Mindfulness were correlated directly with cognitive flexibility and attentional functioning.

As we have seen in Part I, individuals are capable of coping with normal life stressors as well as the ability to work productively. Mental health is very much linked to the other petals and in fact it is often the only aspect of 'health' that the press and media talk about. Our behaviours are influenced by our thoughts and emotions and these in turn affect our social interactions.

Specific tools for the teacher:

Exercise 1 – Mindful breathing – Quick one-minute exercise

Put the timer on your phone on for one minute. Focus on your breath and count every out breath as follows: in… out: one, in… out: two until you reach ten without being distracted by a thought, emotion, or sensation. If you get distracted, simply start again at one.

How was this exercise? Useful?

Exercise 2 – Breathing meditation MP3

Everyone breathes and can use their breath as the focal point of their meditation. Most of the time, we breathe and we're not aware of it. Breathing is regulated by our automatic nervous system and it is only when and if I ask you to become aware of your breath as you read this that you will. We tend to be too busy with our thoughts, emotions and our activities to notice our breath.

This meditation on the breath will not only be dealing with the air coming in and out of the lungs, it will also enable us to become aware of the sensations of that breath as it enters and leaves our body.

This meditation is also extremely beneficial because it will enable us to stop distractions and to make our mind clearer and more focused. Our breath becomes the anchor of the distracted ship of our mind. It keeps us firmly IN THE PRESENT/ IN THE NOW. We do not rush to the past or to the future. It is the focus and we bring our attention back to our breath, over and over again. Very often when we are stressed or anxious, we tend to hold our breath or do very shallow breathing. It is important to take deep breaths to anchor ourselves in the present moment.

At first our mind may seem to be very busy and we might even feel that it is becoming busier. We are becoming more aware of how busy our mind actually is. There will be a great temptation to follow all the thoughts that arise but we should always try and bring our attention back to the breath and focus on it single-pointedly. If we discover that our mind has wandered off and is following a thought, we should bring it back to the natural sensation of the breath, over and over again. We should repeat this as many times as necessary until the mind focuses on the breath.

This meditation should be practised daily – either first thing in the morning or last thing at night and will become the bedrock of our practice.

However, it would be extremely good to remember your breath throughout the day and to focus on it for a minute or so when you get into the car first thing in the morning, when you make a cup of tea, before sending an email... There are many opportunities to include this activity in our daily life.

When there is a storm, the sea or the ocean becomes rough. Sediment is being churned up and the water becomes murky but when the wind dies down the sediments settle and the water becomes clear. In the same way, when the breath calms down the constant flow of thoughts, our mind becomes clear and peaceful.

Mindfulness and meditation on thoughts MP3

The Buddha said 'your worst enemy cannot harm you as much as your unguarded thoughts'. This meditation will therefore get us to notice our thoughts without engaging with them so that we can become more attentive to our thoughts as they come and go, more comfortable with the idea of engaging with each thought or not and more attuned with oneself and others.

Now have a go:

Ensure that you have your feet flat on the floor or if you are doing this lying down that your back is straight, shoulders gently relaxed. Gently close your eyes. If you don't feel comfortable closing your eyes, just focus your gaze about one metre away from you – a gentle gaze. Start by listening to the sounds around you. Then focus – you are focused on what you can hear around you. We are not making up stories about these sounds. We simply notice, acknowledge and welcome them and then let them go and move to the following sound we can hear. If your mind has gone off on a tangent or you are being distracted by a thought, a sensation in your body or an emotion, simply become aware, notice, acknowledge the object of distraction and bring your attention back to the sounds. You do this over and over again. That's the practice. Now bring your attention inwards. Notice where you feel the sensation of your breath the most in your body. The natural flow of your breath. Is it the rising and falling of your chest or abdomen or the slightly cooler air as it comes in through your nostrils and warmer air as you breathe out? It is your breath and your body so there is no right or wrong way of doing this. You know what works best for you. Now, simply focus your attention on your breath – this breath, not the last one nor the next one. The breath becomes the anchor of the distracted ship of our mind. Thoughts, sounds, sensations, emotions will try and hijack our meditation. This is completely normal. Just like with the sounds, you simply need to notice, acknowledge and let them go and bring your attention to the breath. You do this over and over again. I would recommend starting with a three- or five-minute meditation. If you are doing this by yourself, you can use a timer to let you know when the time is up. If you are finding that your mind is really busy, you can count each outbreath (as in exercise 1).

You can download the MP3 by visiting our website.

Physical health

Without our body, we would not be having a physical experience. It is therefore extremely important to learn to take care of our body and ourselves. In 2001, The Department of Health advised adults to be active daily and to do a minimum of 30 minutes moderate intensity activity per day or two hours per week.

Warburton et al. (2006) state that there is irrefutable evidence of the effectiveness of regular physical activity in the primary and secondary prevention of several chronic diseases (e.g. cardiovascular disease, diabetes, cancer, hypertension, obesity, depression and osteoporosis) and premature death.

These activities involve exercise and physical activity focusing on strength, flexibility and endurance. These could be leisurely activities such as walking or cycling and structured exercise (strength training, running or sport).

Physical health also includes nutrition and diet, our nutrient intake, fluid intake and to ensure that we have a healthy digestion.

Recommendations for a healthy diet suggests that it should contain a balanced amount of nutrients such as carbohydrates, proteins, fats, vitamins and minerals.

Physically healthy individuals tend to avoid or reduce their consumption of alcohol and drugs as they report being conscious of the effect of these in their life.

They also practice self-care, which means looking after themselves when they have a cold or they are unwell ensuring that they rest and drink plenty of water, for example.

Many researchers suggest that having between seven and eight hours of undisturbed sleep is the answer to well-being. Rest and sleep did form an important part of the students' daily activities when I interviewed them. They demonstrated when I talked to them that they were conscious that having a good sleep and rest hygiene helped them to be and stay physically healthy.

Students could also clearly recognize that there is a difference between a resourceful and unresourceful state or behaviour and they seemed to be able to identify healthy and unhealthy coping strategies.

For example, one student declared that when she was at the height of her stress, she drank a whole bottle of wine to herself every single night. Initially, she didn't see that it was 'an unresourceful behaviour' but with time and as we talked she became aware of the notion that 'behind every behaviour is a positive intent' and that she was using her drinking as a way to relieve some of her stress and anxiety. She decided to change this habit by going to the gym, for a walk or by having a cup of tea instead. Of course, it was not easy to do but she has since reported being more able to consciously choose whether she has a drink or not. Not simply because it is something she always does when she gets back from university, after a stressful day, but because she really wants to. She also tries to enjoy the glass of wine much more.

Specific tools for the teacher:

Exercise 1 – Mindfulness and walking meditation – movement meditation

Walking meditation is an example of bringing Mindfulness into daily activities. It is a very simple technique that we can engage in every day and experience immediate results of what it means to be in the present moment.

The same principles can be applied to all the movements you make – when you move your arms or when you sit down. The essence is to bring Mindfulness into an act that normally we do quite mechanically and automatically. Very often when we are walking, we are completely focused on what we are going to say when we get there and what we imagine the other person is going to say and what we will respond to them. Or, we are completely focused on what happened in a previous situation, ruminating and rehashing old thoughts. Thus, we miss the experience of going from A to B. Everything that is going on around us in the moment: the trees, the people around us.

In this exercise, we bring awareness into the body. We bring our attention to this current moment and the experience we are having. We focus on the movements. We will do this practice with our eyes open. We can be in touch with all the sensations in our body and at the same time, practice what we have learned and be aware of the sounds around us, the people around us and so on.

We bring our energy down. We don't look at our feet. We just experience our feet from our feet.

Now have a go:

Read the following instructions and then try this exercise for yourself:

Find a comfortable position with your feet flat on the floor. We will be doing this exercise standing up but as it is a movement meditation, it can be used with any movement you make. You can even use this when you brush your teeth. Simply focus on the movement of the toothbrush on each tooth and your hand gestures.

Gently close your eyes and take a nice deep breath. We will start this exercise by 'decomposing' our walking and noticing how many of the movements required to walk are automated in our lives. Of course, this is a good thing, as we wouldn't want to have to think about every single step we take, as it would use up too much of our energy. Now imagine you are about to take a step forward so notice how the weight of your body shifts to one leg, notice how your balance is affected and then put your foot forward and down and take a second step with the other leg. Play around with this exercise for a while, with your eyes open first and then with your eyes closed. Become aware of what is going on inside your body.

Once you have done this, you can start walking around – it can be indoors or outside. Simply focus on the following: lift, shift, forward, step, lift, shift, forward, step, etc.

Walk slowly and focus on feeling your feet from your feet rather than from the 'thought' of your feet.

If outside, you may get distracted by what you can hear (birds singing) or see or by your thoughts and emotions. In the same way as we did with the other exercises, we simply bring our attention back to each step. Not the one we have just taken or the next one but this one, in the present moment and in the now because that is the only guarantee we have in life.

You can download the MP3 by visiting our website.

Exercise 2 – Mindful eating/drinking – how to appreciate our food and drinks

How often do you actually eat your sandwiches whilst working at your desk or drink your cup of tea/coffee whilst getting on with some work or watching TV?

We eat and drink every day so it is good to use these opportunities to gain an experience of the present moment. This exercise encourages us to let go of our mobiles, and other distractions. We put them down and focus solely on one thing: what we are about to eat or to drink and nothing else.

Now you have a go:

Take a piece of chocolate – if it is wrapped take some time opening it. Think about how many people were involved to get this chocolate in your hand and send them all your thanks for making it possible. Now put the chocolate in your hand. Notice any urges or thoughts that come up. Do you feel like eating it quickly? Pick it up and smell it. What can you smell? Does it make your mouth water? Think about the ingredients – cocoa beans – where are they from? Who picked them? And so on, and again bring gratitude for the sun, the rain as well as all the resources and people required to make this piece of chocolate.

Finally, put the piece of chocolate in your mouth and simply let it melt slowly. Notice the flavours in your mouth and any 'mental chatter' going on. Bring you attention back to the sensations. When you have finished eating the piece of chocolate, open your eyes.

Notice how you are feeling? Do you want to eat another piece or another chocolate?

Very often when we eat or drink mindfully we do not want to eat a whole bar of chocolate in five seconds. We start really appreciating what we put in our mouths.

This exercise can be done every time you drink or eat something.

In my workshop, I often also include a raisin for mindful eating and I go through exactly the same steps.

You can download the MP3 by visiting our website.

Exercise 3 – Simple health questionnaire – how to make students aware of their habits

This simple health questionnaire encourages students to reflect on and become aware of their habits. It asks them simple questions about their physical activities, the amount of alcohol/drugs they consume every week, etc. The aim is not to make them feel bad or guilty but to really encourage them to make changes in their daily routine to introduce more physical and healthier activities and habits.

Now you have a go:

On a scale of one to ten (one being never or very rarely and ten being always or almost always) answer the following questions:

Physical activities	
I always have a high level of physical energy	Scale: 1 2 3 4 5 6 7 8 9 10
When I wake up, I feel rested and ready for a new day	Scale: 1 2 3 4 5 6 7 8 9 10
I like exercises and do so regularly every week	Scale: 1 2 3 4 5 6 7 8 9 10
My eating and drinking habits are healthy	Scale: 1 2 3 4 5 6 7 8 9 10
My routines for exercising are well set up	Scale: 1 2 3 4 5 6 7 8 9 10
I have regular 'rests' where I simply 'am'	Scale: 1 2 3 4 5 6 7 8 9 10
I sleep at least seven hours almost every day	Scale: 1 2 3 4 5 6 7 8 9 10
I feel fit and healthy	Scale: 1 2 3 4 5 6 7 8 9 10
I know what to do to recharge my batteries	Scale: 1 2 3 4 5 6 7 8 9 10
Mental activities	
I find it easy to concentrate and focus on my work	Scale: 1 2 3 4 5 6 7 8 9 10
I manage my time effectively and well	Scale: 1 2 3 4 5 6 7 8 9 10
I have a positive outlook on life	Scale: 1 2 3 4 5 6 7 8 9 10
I try to find solutions to problems and issues	Scale: 1 2 3 4 5 6 7 8 9 10
I can easily switch off when not studying/working	Scale: 1 2 3 4 5 6 7 8 9 10
I like to think about things	Scale: 1 2 3 4 5 6 7 8 9 10
Emotional/social activities	
I can recognize my positive and negative emotions	Scale: 1 2 3 4 5 6 7 8 9 10
I am happy with all my emotions and welcome them	Scale: 1 2 3 4 5 6 7 8 9 10
I create good relationships with others	Scale: 1 2 3 4 5 6 7 8 9 10
I get along with my friends	Scale: 1 2 3 4 5 6 7 8 9 10
I get along with my family	Scale: 1 2 3 4 5 6 7 8 9 10
I feel confident	Scale: 1 2 3 4 5 6 7 8 9 10
I feel that I can share with others easily	Scale: 1 2 3 4 5 6 7 8 9 10
I can manage conflict and focus on a positive outcome for all involved	Scale: 1 2 3 4 5 6 7 8 9 10
Spiritual activities	
I have a passion I engage with on a regular basis	Scale: 1 2 3 4 5 6 7 8 9 10
I know what I want to achieve in life	Scale: 1 2 3 4 5 6 7 8 9 10
I have a sense of purpose in life	Scale: 1 2 3 4 5 6 7 8 9 10
I know what my personal values are in life	Scale: 1 2 3 4 5 6 7 8 9 10
I set goals which are aligned with these personal values	Scale: 1 2 3 4 5 6 7 8 9 10
I have a fulfilling life	Scale: 1 2 3 4 5 6 7 8 9 10
I enjoy reconnecting to nature	Scale: 1 2 3 4 5 6 7 8 9 10
I am learning and growing every day	Scale: 1 2 3 4 5 6 7 8 9 10
I am a compassionate human being	

You can download the PDF by visiting our website.

Exercise 4 – Identification of resourceful and unresourceful coping strategies

Once they have filled in the questionnaire, students are encouraged to identify their healthy and unhealthy coping strategies. What do they do when they are feeling stressed? Go out and drink alcohol, use drugs, stay in and don't talk to others? It will enable them to be honest and open and to really look at their behaviours in a different light. Remind them that these behaviours are not bad nor good, they are just coping strategies which I would simply call unresourceful and it is possible to find another strategy which is much more resourceful.

Social health

In the *Sane Society*, Fromm (2001) explains that all human beings have 'the need for relatedness, transcendence, rootedness, the need for a sense of identity and the need for a frame or orientation and devotion' (p.13).

Students that I would describe as flourishing surround themselves with supportive people and possess the ability to develop satisfying interpersonal relationships with others. During our conversations, they also reported more ability to adapt comfortably to various social settings and act appropriately in a variety of situations.

On the other hand, students who would be considered as 'languishing' reported feeling lonely and not feeling part of a community and felt unable to create meaningful relationships. They often feel isolated and cannot see or recognize how they are contributing or making an impact on the community. They also report feeling being different and invisible to others. This is particularly heightened when they come from a different educational background or class.

It is extremely important for students and Higher Education Institutions to be conscious of this aspect. When first-year students transition from secondary school to university they arrive in a completely new environment and are put in halls of residence or in accommodation with people they don't know. If students are unable to form satisfying interpersonal relationships with others where they live and on their course, this will have a very detrimental effect on their university experience and student life. This sets up a bad and negative experience with the 'university'. Some languishing students said that at times they feel that 'no one here cares about me'.

There is a clear need for institutions and for students to ensure that they are integrated into the community the university represents. When I talked with students, they talked about the impact of exclusion (whether real or imagined) on their well-being and on their achievements at university. For example, two or three students I interviewed insisted on the issues they experienced when they first arrived at university and were told that there was no space in halls for them and were put in accommodation with postgraduate students with whom they had nothing in common. Students highlighted the importance of having a sense of belonging at university. They told me that initially they didn't have this sense of belonging because they were so frightened and felt that they didn't fit in. They were worried that no one was going to understand how they were feeling and how much they dreaded the loneliness. Peplau and Perlman (1982) defined loneliness as the aversive state experienced when a discrepancy exists between the interpersonal relationships one wishes to have, and those that one perceives one currently has.

Students I talked to also expressed the fact that when they are feeling stressed or reporting feeling stressed, it becomes a threat to healthy relationship and it prevented them from going out and socializing thus turning the situation into a vicious circle. They reported a focus on themselves rather than on others. Some students also mentioned the fact that when they are having a difficult time, they do not really want to talk to others about their situation or their experience, they simply want to sleep or be on their own. Therefore there's a real focus on the self, versus focus on others.

Fromm-Reichmann (1959, p.3) sheds a light on these feelings and help us understand where they stem from when he states that:

> the longing for interpersonal intimacy stays with every human being from infancy throughout life; and there is no human being who is not threatened by its loss… the human being is born with the need for contact and tenderness.

Strong social skills and good communication skills are required by students to flourish. Training and tips on how to develop such skills would be beneficial to students.

Mindfulness may also help us as academic tutors to develop empathy towards our students and in turn for students to develop self-empathy and empathy for others.

In 2006, Aiken carried out a qualitative study of therapists who were experienced meditators and found that they believed that Mindfulness meditation helped develop empathy towards clients. In particular, interviews were conducted with six psychotherapists who each had more than ten years of experience practising both therapy and Mindfulness meditation. Consistent themes from the data indicated that Mindfulness helps therapists develop their ability to experience and communicate a felt sense of clients' inner experiences; be more present to clients' suffering and help clients express their bodily sensations and feelings.

This same practice may also enable students to learn to be more accepting of the situation, of others and how they behave without wanting to change who they are. It may also enable them to take responsibility for their feelings and gain a sense of accountability.

Research suggests that cooperation may motivate prosocial behaviour by influencing psychological states that support generosity and cooperation. For example, Dunn and Schweitzer (2005, Study 3) found that participants who described a time in the past when they felt grateful towards someone (thereby creating grateful emotion in the present) subsequently reported higher levels of trust towards a third party than did participants who were asked to describe a time they felt angry, guilty or proud.

Emmons and McCullough (2003) also found that participants who wrote daily for two weeks about things for which they were grateful reported offering more emotional support and (with near-statistical significance) tangible help to others than did participants who wrote about their daily hassles or about ways in which they were more fortunate than others.

If the effects of gratitude on psychological well-being (Emmons and McCullough 2003) are due to real (or even merely perceived) changes in people's social relationships and if positive social relations are conducive to health and well-being, then Mindfulness and the gratitude meditation might be a good activity for students and members of staff alike.

Specific tools for the teacher:

Exercise 1 – Mindfulness and gratitude meditation – developing gratitude for everything/everyone in your life

Cicero stated that 'Gratitude is not only the greatest of the virtues but the parent of all others.' (2004, p.37)

If we reflect on what we don't have, this leads to unhappiness. This meditation will do the opposite and will encourage us to focus on all the positive aspects in our life. Our experience of happiness in the world depends upon the response that we give to our life and our life events, not what is actually happening in our life. It is all down to our state of mind and mental habits.

Nothing less, nothing more. We can increase our experience of happiness not necessarily by manipulating our external environment but simply by changing our mind and most importantly by focusing on all the good things we possess or experience.

Now you have a go:

Find a comfortable position with your feet flat on the floor. Gently close your eyes and take a nice deep breath. And again. For a minute or so focus on the sounds around you (same exercise as mindful awareness). Now, bring your attention inwards and focus on your breath, wherever you feel it the most in your body. For a minute focus on the sensation of the natural flow of your breath coming in and out of your body. Now, we will start with the gratitude practice. We focus on our body and we think about all the parts of our body we are grateful for (our hands, legs, the sense of touch, smell, hearing, particularly if we are lucky enough to be able to use these unaided).

We then start focusing on all the people in our lives we are grateful for – our loved ones, our close relatives and family, our friends and colleagues, acquaintances, people we meet in the street and even people who represent a challenge for us. Notice what sensations gratitude generates in your body. When we feel genuinely grateful for things/people in our lives, it creates a lovely sensation in our bodies.

You can download the MP3 by visiting our website.

Exercise 2 - The gratitude daily challenge

As mentioned before, gratitude helps us feel happier and appreciating what we have in our life really helps. This gratitude daily challenge involves a quick exercise every morning and afternoon. Simply spend several mornings when you first wake up and last thing at night to find three to five new things to be grateful for every day. It helps to also do it at the end of the day and to review what went well in your day, what you would do differently and to focus on specific events and people.

Again, focus on the sensation that this gratitude produces in your body.

Spiritual health

Egan et al. (2011) declared that 'spirituality means different things to different people. It may include (a search for) one's ultimate beliefs and values, a sense of meaning and purpose in life, a sense of connectedness, identity and awareness and for some people religion.' (p.309)

Banks (1998) referred to the principle of Universal Mind to explain 'spiritual health' and describes it as the formless energy that animates all of life – the intelligent life energy behind human psychological functioning.

For me, spiritual health is linked to the sense we give to things and life. There is something more than just getting up in the morning, going to work, eating and then going to bed. There is a deeper sense to our existence. Maybe it could be described as a sense of belonging to something bigger? Our society has standards and ideas of success, which suggest that to be happy we need to get the degree, get the job, get the car, then get a better job with more money, get a house, get married, etc. There is a sense of emptiness when we realize that a good job, good money, a big house and car with lots of holidays does not mean that we will be happy. It gives some of us a sense of emptiness because we lack a sense of purpose and a life mission. Some students said that they often asked themselves – why am I here? What do I love and what impact do I want to make with my life?

Macmin and Foskett (2004) highlight the fact that spirituality is an issue that individuals and communities are asking to be recognized in various contexts and in particular mental health.

Spiritual health is a personal matter involving values and beliefs that provide a purpose in our lives. While different individuals may have different views of what spiritual health is, it is generally considered to be the search for meaning and purpose in human existence. It leads us to strive for a state of harmony with ourselves, and others, and a balance between our inner needs and the rest of the world.

This spiritual health can be linked to religion or to the idea that there is something bigger than us. It can also simply be a need to be connected to nature and be outside (in a field, a forest, etc.) but most importantly it is that sense of knowing that there are things we would like to achieve in life. An area of interest or topics for which we have developed a real passion and that we can imagine ourselves spending a lot of time doing (even if we are not paid for it).

Spiritual health also leads to compassion as it makes us appreciate what we have in our lives and the advantages we have in comparison to others.

Specific tools for the teacher:

Exercise 1 - Life purpose exercise

This exercise involves sitting down and thinking about the type of life you truly want. It can be done once a year or more regularly – every three or six months. It can be done on your own or by enlisting the help of someone else and consists of identifying several time frames (short/medium/long term) and all the areas of your life you would like to explore (e.g. professional/financial/family, etc.)

Now you have a go:

Areas of your life	Short term	Medium term	Long term
University	Write plan for essay	Write 2,000-word essay for end of term	Pass my first year with 2:1 overall grades.

You can download the PDF by visiting our website.

Exercise 2 – Mindfulness and meditation on Loving Kindness – bringing compassion to oneself and others

The Dalai Lama said that 'love and compassion are necessities, not luxuries. Without them humanity cannot survive.' (1999, p.59) This meditation is also called Metta. This is the Sanskrit word for the practice of Loving Kindness. We simply develop the wish for everyone to be happy, including ourselves. This is also called compassion and to apply true compassion we need to commit and to apply it to everyone and everything around us. Our compassionate attitude does not change when we believe someone is behaving in a negative way. It is a mental attitude based on the wish for others to be free from their suffering and to be able to overcome their problems. It is also linked to a sense of commitment, responsibility and respect towards others.

We develop a state of mind that can include a wish for good things for oneself. In developing Loving Kindness or compassion, we begin with the wish to be free of suffering and then take that natural feeling towards oneself and cultivate it, enhance it and extend it out to include and encompass others.

Now have a go:

Read the following instructions and then try this exercise for yourself:

Find a comfortable position with your feet flat on the floor. Gently close your eyes and take a nice deep breath. And again. For a minute or so focus on the sounds around you (same exercise as mindful awareness). Now, bring your attention inwards and focus on your breath, wherever you feel it the most in your body. For a minute focus on the sensation of the natural flow of your breath coming in and out of your body. Now, we will start with a specific mantra. We start with ourselves because if we are suffering, we cannot help anybody else and we say: 'may I be secure, be happy, be healthy, live well'. We repeat this for a minute or so and then we bring up someone whom we love or respect greatly and we say 'may you be secure, be happy, be healthy, live well'. We then extend this to a work colleague or someone we know but not as well, we then do the same with someone we find challenging and with whom we don't really get on with. If we are unable to send them good wishes, then at this point, we are the one suffering and the one in need for loving kindness and compassion and so we say again: 'may I be secure, be happy, be healthy, live well'. The person we don't get on with is not here with us and they are probably unaware that we have these feelings or emotions towards them so what is the point of keeping them inside ourselves as we are punishing ourselves instead? Nelson Mandela said it beautifully: 'Resentment is like drinking/taking poison and then hoping it will kill your enemies.'

We finish this exercise by sending loving kindness to everybody around us – in front of us, behind us, to the sides (left and right), above and below us (this also includes animals) by saying: 'may you all be secure, be happy, be healthy, live well'.

You can download the MP3 by visiting our website.

Openness

Openness refers both to experiences and people. It means that we are interested in discovering and experiencing new and different things than we have in the past. We also tend to be interested in others and to be more open to who they are, what they do and their beliefs or values. If we go back to the metaphor of the flower, it suggests that as a flower we accept the other flowers standing next to us or in the garden.

Recent studies have indicated that factors other than intelligence, such as two out of the Big Five personality traits (conscientiousness and openness), are useful predictors of academic performance (Chamorro-Premuzic and Furnham, 2003a, 2003b).

McCrae and Costa's (1987) Five Factor Model measures broad factors such as openness to experience and reported that the following adjectives best characterize openness: 'original, imaginative, broad interests and daring' (p.87).

Students who participated in my eight-week Mindfulness workshops reported being more open to others and to diverse experiences. For example, one student in particular stated that they were more engaged with the challenges they were faced with, knowing that they would not be there forever and being more able to receive information about themselves (e.g. getting feedback) and thus reporting feeling less defensive and most importantly being able to maintain greater emotional balance when faced with stressful and difficult situations as well as noticing their negative thoughts and emotions and being able to distance themselves from them rather than automatically engaging and identifying with them.

Curiosity

What is curiosity?

Curiosity is defined by the Oxford Dictionary as 'a strong desire to learn or know something'.

Being curious was expressed by students I interviewed and colleagues as a real desire to know, to understand. A way of thinking that motivates us to go deeper, to analyse topics and concepts and to show interest. It was also described by a colleague in particular as a way of questioning what is established by going beyond appearances and fixed concepts. Being curious is part of this thirst to learn, this thirst to discover, to be faced with something new, to question facts and to look for new information, to observe and analyse.

The attributes of curious young people

The students who described themselves as curious also stated that they felt enthusiasm, a real desire to learn and discover new things, interest and even passion for the topic they studied at university. We can be curious about our culture, our beliefs, our differences and similarities, how things function and how useful they are or not. We can also question how certain aspects have a specific place in our lives and how we create them.

During the interviews carried out for this book, it would appear that curious students have a clear motivation to discover more about their topic and their chosen field of study. They want to discover interesting facts and concepts and are not afraid to ask questions.

Flexibility

What is flexibility?

The term flexibility is defined by the Oxford dictionary as: 'The quality of bending easily without breaking. The ability to be easily modified. The willingness to change or compromise.'

Flexibility and adaptability seem to be two major competences that flourishing students possess. When I interviewed some students, who were performing very well academically, they indicated that they learned very early on in their university life that these were two of the most important qualities a student must have. They also stated that they were both willing to change with or without notice and that they developed the ability to adapt to change (in their environment, their daily schedule and routine). The willingness to modify the way they worked through feedback was also something that flourishing students mentioned. They said it was difficult to receive feedback from tutors and at times even intimidating but that when they moved past the notion that it was a daunting task, they quickly realized that to perform better they had to receive feedback and integrate it into their next piece of work.

Most importantly, the flexibility also requires a willingness to recognize the need for help and to accept it. Flexible students are happy to look for different solutions to their problems.

Resilience

What is resilience?

The term resilience stems from Latin (*resiliens*) and was originally used to refer to the pliant or elastic quality of a substance (Joseph 1994).

The Oxford Dictionary defines resilience as 'The capacity to recover quickly from difficulties; toughness' or 'the ability of a substance or object to spring back into shape; elasticity.'

I am not particularly keen on this definition because from my own experience, the changes didn't happen 'quickly' but over time. The same seems to be true about the students who shared their stories of resilience. There is also an issue with the idea of 'springing back into shape', as it would mean that the person reverts to their own 'state of being' without experiencing any personal and developmental changes.

My favourite definition is that of the American Psychological Association which describes resilience as 'the process of adapting well in the face of adversity, trauma, tragedy, threats or significant sources of stress — such as family and relationship problems, serious health problems or workplace and financial stressors. It means "bouncing back" from difficult experiences.'[23]

The attributes of resilient young people

Benard (1991) argues that we are all born with innate resiliency, with the capacity to develop the traits commonly found in resilient survivors.

- *Social competence* (responsiveness, cultural flexibility, empathy, caring, communication skills and a sense of humour). She describes social competence as the ability to elicit positive responses from others, thus establishing positive relationships with both adults and peers.
- *Problem-solving* (planning, help-seeking, critical and creative thinking); or the planning that facilitates seeing oneself in control and resourcefulness in seeking help from others.
- *Autonomy* (sense of identity, self-efficacy, self-awareness, task-mastery and adaptive distancing from negative messages and conditions); or a sense of one's own identity and an ability to act independently and exert some control over one's environment.
- *A sense of purpose and belief in a bright future* (goals, educational aspirations, persistence, hopefulness and a sense of a bright future).

Resilience is not a genetic trait that only a few of us possess but it is our inborn capacity for self-righting (Werner and Smith 1992), transformation and change (Lifton 1993) Werner and Smith also declared that a resilient child is one 'who loves well, works well, plays well, and expects well' (p.192).

---

23 www.apa.org/helpcenter/road-resilience.aspx

Resilience is really what helps us have a better than expected outcome after a difficult event.

Resilience is generating protective factors or processes when facing difficulty and so it is much more something we do than something we have.

In the book *Second wave positive psychology* Ivtzan et al. (2015) talk about three meanings of resilience:

a) Resistance resilience is being strong in the face of adversity.

b) Recovering resilience is being able to recover from adversity.

c) Reconfiguration resilience is where we are transformed by adversity in ways that bring benefits. This is also known as post-traumatic growth.

Differences between resilient and non-resilient people

There is neurological evidence to support the psychological data that show some people may be relatively high or low in resilience (Waugh et al. 2008)

Waugh et al. found that when people with higher resilience were shown a cue signalling there was an equal chance they would see a distressing picture or neutral picture, they only exhibited neural reactions indicating an unpleasant emotional response if they actually saw the distressing picture. Resilient people also returned to baseline cardiac and neurological states sooner than those with low resilience when exposed to stressful situations (Waugh et al. 2008).

In contrast, participants with low resilience reacted to threats or even a possibility of threats sooner and for longer periods of time, as indicated by activity in the amygdala and insular areas of the brain (Waugh et al. 2008).

As academic tutors and members of staff, we can help our students change this. Neuroplasticity can be our ally. We can explain to students that neuroplasticity enables the brain to create new neural pathways by creating new connections between our neurons. Our brain then uses these pathways to act. They are installed through learning, education and by developing new habits. This means that it is possible for students to become more resilient.

Language

The language we use daily contributes to the way we interact with others and the world around us. Our words and expressions influence both our attitude and behaviours towards a situation or a person. The ability to speak is a power. With our words, we can do a lot of damage or we can soothe. We need to be aware and to discover the vocabulary we use and what impact it has on our body, mind and on others.

Useful presuppositions

When I trained as an NLP practitioner and Master practitioner, I was introduced to the NLP presuppositions. They form the central principles of NLP and come across in our lives through the language we use and our choices of words. They can be considered as the guiding philosophy or 'beliefs'. NLP does not claim that they are true or universal but they see them as a very useful 'working principle' to have in our life. Because we presuppose they are true, we act as if they were and we start introducing them in our life. When I interviewed students and experts, although they did not 'voice' or 'express' these concepts in exactly this way, some of these presuppositions are helpful for students and can help them flourish.

Here are some of them.

- *People respond to their experience, not to reality itself. The map is not the territory.*

We do not know what reality is. Our senses, beliefs and past experience give us a map of the world from which to operate. But a map is never completely accurate otherwise it would be the same as the ground it covers. So, for example, a map of London is not the city of London itself. It is just a representation of its streets. Some maps are better than others for finding our way round. We will look at this in more detail when we talk about communication models and how we filter the information we receive.

- *Having a choice is better than not having a choice.*

Always try to have a map of the world that gives you the widest number of choices. If you have no choice, you are dead. If you have two choices, you have a dilemma, if you have three choices or more, you have options. You will be freer as a result and have the ability to influence your life more.

- *People make the best choice they can at all times.*

We always do the best we can with the resources we have in the moment. These choices may appear as bizarre, unhelpful or evil to others but that might be the only way we can cope with a situation at a given point based on our 'maps of the world'. If we are given more choices or options, we can take them and change our behaviours and ways of thinking. I believe this is a particularly useful concept, as it reduces feelings of guilt and self-blame.

- *People work perfectly.*

Nobody is broken or wrong. Nobody needs mending. We are all executing our strategies effectively. Some of our strategies may be flawed or ineffective but it can be changed to something more useful and desirable.

- *All actions have a purpose.*

Our actions are not random. We are always trying to achieve something, although we may not be aware of what it is.

- *Every behaviour has a positive intention.*

All our actions have at least one purpose – to make us happy. We tend to do things that we value and that benefit us. NLP separates the intention behind the action and the action itself. A person is not their behaviour. When a person has a better choice of behaviour that also achieves their positive intention, they will take it.

- *The unconscious mind balances the conscious; it is not malicious.*

The unconscious is everything that is not in consciousness at the present moment. It contains all the resources we need to live in balance.

- *The meaning of the communication is not simply what you intend, but also the response you get.*

The response you get from communication may be different from the one you wanted, but there are no failures in communication, only responses and feedback. If you are not getting the results you want, change what you are doing. Take responsibility for the way you communicate and for the result it creates.

- *We already have all the resources we need or we can create them.*

There are no unresourceful people, only unresourceful states of mind and they can be changed if we are aware of them.

- *Mind and body form a system. They are different expressions of one person.*

Mind and body interact and influence each other. It is not possible to make a change in one without the other being affected. When we think differently, our bodies change. When we act differently, we change our thoughts and our emotions (see neuroplasticity).

- *We process all information through our senses.*

Developing your senses so that they become more accurate gives you better information and helps you think more clearly.

- *Modelling successful performance leads to excellence.*

NLP is the study of excellence and was created by two Americans, John Grinder and Richard Bandler, who modelled three therapists – Virginia Satir (family therapist), Fritz Perls (father of Gestalt Therapy) and Milton Erickson (hypnotherapy). They believed that if one person can do something, then it is possible for another to model it and to teach it to others. In this way, everyone can learn to get better results in their own way. This is a bit what we are doing in this book. You do not become a clone of the person you are modelling, you discover their 'strategies' to deal with a situation or event and you adopt them in your life. You learn from them.

- *If you want to understand, act.*

The learning is in the doing.

- *There are no errors only learning. No mistakes only feedback.*

We do not make mistakes or errors which have a negative connotation. We learn and use the feedback to 'bridge the gap' between where we are and where we want to be.

- *If you always do what you've always done, then you will always get what you've always got.*

Pretty self-explanatory – if you carry on doing the same thing all the time, you will get the same results all the time.

- *It's not what happens to you that matters to you but what you do with it.*

How we communicate

The NLP Communication model was developed by Tad James and Wyatt Woodsmall in 1988 based on the work initially produced by Grinder and Bandler in the 1970s. It uses many concepts of Cognitive Psychology and the work of linguists and analysts Alfred Korzybski (1933) and Noam Chomsky (1964).

We are constantly taking in information through our five senses and processing it. A lot of the information we receive takes place unconsciously. Consciously trying to process all the data received would not be possible and would require us to use too much energy. Therefore, our nervous system filters it.

The filters we use are based on the language we use, the words we use, our beliefs, memories, our unique experience (what happened to us in the past), our metaprograms. Everyone filters and experiences any given situation differently. It's our internal representations (subjective perceptions) that determine how we view the world and everything we experience.

We then delete, distort or generalize information per our unique filters.

Once incoming information passes through our filters, a thought is constructed. These thoughts create internal representations (or maps of the world). For example – read this and then close your eyes and try it out:

Think of a lemon – imagine that you have it in your hands and feel how heavy or light it is. Then take it up to your nose and smell it. Can you smell it? Now take a knife and hear the noise it makes as you cut it in half – notice the strong smell coming out of it. How do you feel? Now take one half and put it in your mouth. Taste the bitterness in your mouth. Remember last time you had a lemon like this.

This example demonstrates that we form internal representations which are effectively sensory perceptions such as a picture with sounds, emotions, smells and tastes. Our internal representations immediately trigger corresponding emotions or 'states' as we call them in NLP jargon, which then impact on all our behaviours and on our physiology.

So, the reality that we experience is largely determined by what we do inside our heads.

Our language – a way of expressing our map of the world.

Observing your language or that of your students/colleagues might give you an indication of their preferences. Here are some examples:

Visual

I get the picture… I see what you mean… let's get this in perspective… it appears that… show me… the focus of attention… take a closer look… looking closer… it's clear to me… a different angle… this is the outlook… with hindsight… you'll look back on this.

Auditory

That rings a bell… we're on the same wavelength… let's talk about it… within earshot… let's discuss things… I'm speechless… shout from the hilltops… people will hear you… this silence is deafening… it's music to my ears… word for word… in a manner of speaking.

Kinaesthetic

He's thick skinned… a cool customer… I grasp your meaning… a heated argument… I will be in touch… I can't put my finger on it… we are scratching the surface… let's dig deeper… hit the nail on the head… I feel it in my stomach.

Olfactory/digital

It's a matter of taste… let's chew it over… I smell a rat… it's a bitter pill to swallow… that's an acid comment… it's a bit fishy… it leaves a bad taste.

Being aware of your own sensory preference and that of others can help us communicate better. If someone uses a lot of 'kinaesthetic' language, they are likely to respond better if you use the same language than if you use 'visual' words.

Language difference between the flourishing and the languishing student

During the interviews I carried out with the ten students, I noticed a major difference between the language used by students who were reporting feeling stressed and anxious or those who were not reporting major stress in their life.

> – *I can't versus I can and it's possible as well as 'should versus could'*

When I replayed some of the interviews, I became aware that some students tended to have a much more negative view of the situation and they used modals such as 'I can't' and 'it's not possible' where students who reported feeling more settled and having overcome some of their difficult experiences and situations used words such 'I can' and 'it's possible', 'I am going to try'.

Others tended to use words such as 'I should be doing better', 'I should get on with my assignment or work' whereas others clearly focused on goals and what might be possible when considering future tasks: 'I could start working early'.

The use of words such as 'I can' seems to match the 'conscious autosuggestion technique described by Coué in his books *Self mastery through conscious autosuggestion* (1922) and *How to practice suggestion and autosuggestion* (1923) in which he stated that, 'believing that the thing which you wish to do is easy, it becomes so for you, although it may appear difficult to others.' (1923, pp.77–78).

–   *Self-focused versus other-focused*

There is also a clear difference between the language focus of some students who tend to use I, me, myself, mine and therefore be much more self-focused and others who are much less self-focused and who discuss how their experience impacted on others and how others helped them.

It would be very interesting to explore this aspect further and to see whether these different uses of language impact on a student's ability to flourish in their environment.

- PART III -

THE TUTOR'S OWN TOOLBOX

Chapter 5
It all starts with you –
the flourishing tutor

'Change starts with you'
– Einstein

In many Higher Education Institutions, the vision is to nurture skilled, adaptable and resilient graduates who can thrive in the global economy which is changing faster than ever and this means taking care of the student's well-being so that we can have a 'flourishing student'.

This concept is admirable and makes complete sense but it is also vital for staff to be 'flourishing' in their working environment and to focus on their well-being. There is therefore a real need for a 'positive staff experience' too. If we go back to the flourishing student model, it does not simply apply to students but also to us. We are part of a system and as such our own stress level will affect others around us. Very often, as teachers and tutors, we tend to forget our own health and we don't take care of ourselves as well as we recommend others to do for themselves.

Of course, when I talk with colleagues, it is obvious to me that we all understand that taking time to relax, eat well, to read, to go for a walk or for a massage, all of these things are extremely good for our well-being and that our well-being depends on how we look after ourselves, how kind and gentle we are with ourselves. But sometimes the gap between theory and putting things into practice is too big a jump. There is always one more email we could be answering or something that we haven't quite finished.

But looking after ourselves and our well-being is not selfish. In fact, we often give others most of our attention throughout the day, our loved ones, or our colleagues but we are not prepared to give ourselves some time to simply 'BE' and to rest. When I run my Mindfulness workshops with students and staff, I always remind everyone that we are called 'human beings' not 'human doings' so it is important to BE human from time to time.

The beauty of simply 'being' is that it brings a peaceful feeling that cannot be equalled. It is so easy to achieve yet so difficult in the sense that we often feel that we cannot stop thinking or cannot stop engaging with a given situation. It doesn't take long and once you have developed the habit, it becomes easier and easier.

How is your mental/physical/social/emotional/spiritual health doing?

So, as a member of staff in HE, what is your own level of stress and most importantly are you flourishing or languishing?

Jim Loehr and Tony Schwartz based their research on the consulting they have done with the world's greatest athletes. In their book *The Power of Full Engagement* (2005) they explain that energy, not time, is the fundamental currency of high performance and that it is an even more precious resource that we need to manage well.

On our website www.flourishingstudents.com, you will be able to download an energy management questionnaire which contains 40 questions that will enable you to assess your physical, mental, emotional and core energies (strong sense of purpose built on spiritual values).

This will give you a quick and helpful way to assess how you perform in using these energies and in recharging your batteries for each energy type.

Your role – not in isolation but part of a whole

In life, there are two ways of looking at a situation. We can either choose the simple cause and effect thinking which suggests that for example university life is causing students to become more and more stressed or we can choose to look at it from the lens of Systems Thinking.

Systems Thinking focuses on the whole system and looks at how the various parts of a system interact with each other and through interrelated actions that produce behaviours and results and lead to effects on each other. Senge defines it (1990, p.7) as 'a conceptual framework, a body of knowledge and tools that has been developed to make the full patterns clearer, and to help us see how to change them effectively'.

If we integrate this idea of Systems Thinking we recognize that as members of staff we are part of the problem and part of the solution. It encourages us to look at the issues experienced, try to understand how they have arisen and to gain more understanding and perspective to discover ways to deal with things differently.

In a video explaining what Systems Thinking is,[24] Senge states that it is important for us to have a very deep and persistent commitment to 'learning' and we must be prepared to be wrong. For him, if it was pretty obvious what we ought to

---

24 https://youtu.be/HOPfVVMCwYg

be doing, then we would already be doing it. We are part of the problem – our own way of seeing things, our own sense of where there is leverage, is probably part of the problem too. Our 'mental models' are also an issue. If we are prepared to challenge our own mental models, we are more likely to find leverage and solutions. Finally, we need to triangulate and work collectively. We need to get different people, from different points of view who are seeing different parts of the system to come together and collectively start to see something that individually none of us can see.

This is extremely relevant in the case of the increased stress and anxiety reported by students. If we want to change things and find leverage, we need to work together (students, staff and all members of Higher Education Institutions).

The interviews I carried out with experts, students, and members of staff have confirmed this aspect and have made me even more convinced of the importance of the interaction between all the elements of an institution.

How to create a community instead of an 'institution' which fosters resilience, diversity, inclusion and student voices

During my conversations with students, they expressed the need for inclusion and for their voices to be heard. This is something that also regularly comes up in the National Student Survey (NSS). As we saw previously, Systems Thinking is the answer because it enables us to see our institution as a whole rather than as different parts (students, administrative and professional staff, academic members of staff, etc.) and to acknowledge that we all contribute to this whole system that is a HE Institution, which generates the issues. It is therefore important for all of us to embrace the notion of the university as a garden where each one of us is a flower that will contribute to the overall beauty of the composition. It will also help us fully accept that we all have a role to play to ensure that changes happen and that we have a garden which enables each individual flower to feel part of it but also allowed to fully bloom and fully be itself. Senge in *The fifth discipline* (1990) summarizes this when he says that 'Systems thinking shows us that there is no separate "other"; that you and the someone else are part of a single system. The cure lies in your relationship with your "enemy"' (p.67). When I read this, it really motivates me to connect with others in my institution to see how as a part of the system, I can contribute to improve the situation and create a positive environment for both staff and student to have a great experience.

I hope you also feel inspired.

Chapter 6
Your skills

'You never really understand a person until you consider things from his point of view'
– Harper Lee

Listening skills and empathy

Our students said that they have three major needs: to love, to be loved and to feel secure. This is something all human beings have in common. The students also said that they need to trust us and they need to know that we have their best interests at heart. This trust can best be developed by creating a relationship which is based on the Rogerian Core Conditions.

These conditions do not suggest that we never challenge our students. In fact, challenge is very much part of our work. But I believe that it can be done from the angle of the core conditions. These core conditions are: empathy, unconditional positive regard and congruence.

Carl Rogers (1995) described empathy as:

the ability to perceive the internal frame of reference of another with accuracy, and with the emotional components and meanings which pertain thereto, as if one were the other person but without ever losing the 'as if' condition. Thus, it means to sense the hurt or the pleasure of another as he senses it, and to perceive the causes thereof as he perceives them, but without ever losing the recognition that it is as if I were hurt or pleased etc. If this 'as if' quality is lost, then the state is one of identification. (p.39)

Mindfulness can help us develop the skills we require to be emphatic and good listeners. Two of the skills students need from us when they are experiencing difficulties and want to share with us.

Research and its empirical evidence demonstrate that Mindfulness practice encourages the development of skills that impact on trainees' effectiveness as therapists. In a four-year qualitative study (Newsome et al. 2006; Schure et al. 2008), after taking a 15-week course that included Mindfulness meditation and counselling students reported considerable positive effects on their counselling skills and therapeutic relationships, including being more attentive to the therapy process, more comfortable with silence and more attuned with oneself and clients.

Time

It is important to ensure that the conversations with students are not rushed so that students get a feeling that they're being heard and that they have a space to be heard. It is clear that we all have a lot of work but it is vital that we remain present in the moment with students and that if students come to see us at a time when we are not free, we arrange a longer appointment later. At least two of the ten students I interviewed told me that it made a difference to them when they didn't feel like they were being a 'burden' and when they felt 'heard and understood' by their tutor because it might be the first instance that a student expresses their feelings or talks about their emotions and this could make a big difference to them.

Confidentiality

Confidentiality is central to the creation of trust between students and members of staff. If we want our students to discuss their issues and problems with us but also if we want to be able to help them, it is important that they feel that we are going to keep their information safe and confidential unless there is compelling evidence for us not to. Establish clear ground rules at the start which clearly deal with confidentiality and limits and always follow the procedures set by your institution.

During our work, we will come across a wide range of situations and events that happen to students. We may be tempted to discuss them with fellow colleagues but we need to remember that any information about identifiable students is confidential. It is vital that we therefore take great care in making sure that we do not disclose such information to friends, colleagues or family, unless they are directly involved in the teaching of the student and need to be informed.

Universities have their own rules and regulations about confidentiality and it is important that we know, understand and respect these.

Know your limits – what to say, not to say

We are not health-care experts so it is extremely important that regardless of our impressions of services provided by GPs or other departments in our institutions that we do not give any advice to students which could be detrimental to them.

I often have students who tell me that some tutors have told them not to worry about the way they feel and that it may disappear and who have advised them not to go to see a GP because they are likely to give them antidepressants or vice versa that they should go and see their GP because they would be given something to help them with their condition. I feel that this could potentially be very damaging for the student's health and it also sets expectations and preconceptions which are not good for anyone. As academic tutors, we do not have the relevant training and experience to understand what medication would be beneficial or not to students. Most importantly, we do not have the medical history of our students and we cannot know what they need medically. It is therefore vital that we refrain from sharing our beliefs around medication. As indicated previously, some students will clearly not require any medical treatment but others will and it is important to ensure that we do not make these decisions ourselves but that we let qualified people do it instead.

Boundaries, boundaries, boundaries – do you know where to refer your students?

It may seem pretty obvious to most of us but knowing what services are available within our department, school, faculty and our institution overall is vital.

Most institutions provide amazing pastoral services for students ranging from students' health services, counselling services, vulnerable students' services, senior tutors or mental-health advisers. They may have various names in various settings but what is vital for the students is that as members of staff, we know who the main points of contact are and that we can refer the student confidently. So, how well do you know the services in your university? Do you know who to refer students to and how to 'escalate' if required? Would you be able to explain this clearly to your student?

Guiding rather than leading

Leading suggests that we are taking others in a specific direction and almost telling them where to go and what to do. In the case of students, it would mean leading them in a specific direction or giving them advice to do or not do something specific. It is sometimes tempting to give students specific instructions because we believe we have been in the same situation and we have the answer for them. But the reality is that we are different individuals and that our past experiences and knowledge might not be the best thing they need. From my conversations with students, it is clear that they already know and understand how much they have been led during their studies in their secondary school.

Some students have said that they remember times when their tutors clearly tried to help them by either giving them advice such as 'you need to go home and have a break' or giving their opinion on their situation or by telling them what to do. But they added that these comments, even though they seemed to be given because their tutor cared, did not help them at all. For them, it is better to be presented with options so that they can make an informed choice.

Guiding on the other hand is more about recognizing that the person in front of us knows where they want to go and what outcomes they want to achieve and we guide them and support them in getting there. It may also be that students don't know what they want or where they want to go and our role as guides is to act as a navigation system or support system which will enable the person to get to the best place possible based on some of the wants and needs they are expressing.

This means listening to the person who is experiencing difficulties in a respectful way. This means being non-directive, paying attention and enabling solely for the student to express themselves freely so that they don't feel judged, directed or guided and most importantly without having to hear our comments, our opinions, or our advice nor our personal experiences that we decide to share with them 'because it might be of interest to them'. (But also because, let's be honest, there is always a part of us that likes talking about ourselves but the fact is that students don't care!) To do this effectively, we need to be aware of our unconscious bias too.

The final aim is always to try and give back control to students so that they feel empowered to take responsibility and to choose how they want to deal with a specific situation and become independent and balanced individuals. For example, it is good to leave students with a clear plan and next steps, even if it means that you find out some information for them.

Can you recognize what is going on with your tutees?

How much awareness do you have and can you recognize what is going on with your tutees?

As we have seen before most of the time we cannot modify the events in our own life but most importantly in others' lives. It can be a physical illness, a death, a mental illness. The most challenging aspect is that we cannot act on the way our students are experiencing these stressful events. Every individual goes through life the way they want and we do so depending on our personalities, our past (our roots), our mental models which are all linked to our education, our social cultural environment, our age, our well-being, etc.

The problem with this feeling of powerlessness is that it can make us feel like we are unable to help and it might also make us want to avoid students who are experiencing difficulties because we feel uncomfortable. In our society where we are expected to act and to 'do things', it is difficult for us to simply be there and to listen.

Do your students know that you are not indifferent to their suffering and that you really feel empathy for them?

When we don't know how to show that we care or when we are uncomfortable around students who are experiencing issues, it sends the message to students that we are trying to avoid the situation or to distance ourselves from it and the student may get a sensation of being misunderstood or feeling lonely.

So, are you clear about your intentions when you help students? Having a clear intention is great but what matters is the result. It is important that as academic personal tutors and lecturers we think, observe and question what is going on so that we can become much more aware and conscious to focus on the relationship we establish with our tutees. This means they feel we are truly listening, interested in their situation and respectful of their differences and their experiences. It is sensible to adopt the principle that deep down we don't know this student nor do we fully understand what is happening and that the best way to approach the situation is to be open-minded and present in the here and now.

Chapter 7
How to bridge the student's skill gaps

'What got you here, won't get you there'
– Einstein

Conscious incompetence versus unconscious competence

There is a clear gap between our knowledge of a topic that students have chosen to study at university and their own knowledge. We are what I call 'unconsciously competent' whereas our students are 'consciously incompetent'. Let's have a look at this NLP concept and how it works.

It starts with unconscious incompetence – we don't know that we don't know. Let's use the example of driving a car to explain this further. Before we start taking driving lessons, we are not fully aware of all the skills required to drive a car. This is called unconscious incompetence. When we start having lessons, we become consciously aware of what we don't know – this is the second phase known as conscious incompetence.

We realize that we need to think hard and to concentrate to change gears, use mirrors, turn, etc. As we become better drivers we move on to conscious competence, this means that you 'know what you know' and you are consciously aware of that knowledge. You can change gears or drive more easily but you still need a lot of support from your instructor and need to focus on what you are doing. It might be that once you pass your driving test, you can drive the car on your own and are a 'conscious driver' with conscious competence but you would, for example, find it difficult to drive when a friend in the back of the car is chatting or with the radio on.

The final stage is unconscious competence – you don't know what you know and that you know. You do things almost automatically. At this point, as a driver you can drive miles on the motorway whilst thinking about some of your issues or what you are going to do when you get home or you can drive whilst listening to the radio etc.

As you can see from this example, there is a big gap and difference between conscious incompetence – you are aware of how much you don't know and understand yet and unconscious competence where you know your topic and subject so well that you don't have to think very hard about it. Students arrive at university and usually find themselves in the conscious incompetence/conscious competence zone whereas most of us are unconsciously competent. The problem in that situation is that interactions with students will be based on our beliefs that they also understand things and see things in the same way we do and we may not explain things in as much detail as they might require because we might believe that it is not necessary.

How to bridge the gap between knowledge

We need first to admit to ourselves that this is happening and to acknowledge that whilst we are passionate, motivated and interested in a topic and that we fully understand and know what we talk about, our students arrive with skills and knowledge which are completely different. We also need to be empathetic, as we too were students once and we didn't know as much as we do now.

It is therefore vital to bridge the gap between our knowledge so that students feel motivated and empowered to learn. One way to do so is to use scaffolding, which was first presented by Wood et al. in 1976. The theory is that when students are given the support they need while learning something new, they stand a better chance of using that knowledge independently.

Once we know students understand a concept or a theory, we can then take a step aside and let them work independently or in groups to apply these in context and strengthen and reinforce their knowledge.

Letting go of our own labels/bias – how do you define students' success?

How do you define students' success? How would you define someone who is successful and gets good grades at university? All these concepts have a great impact on how we interact with our students and on how they receive the information we provide them with.

It is extremely important for us to be aware of our unconscious bias. They are 'mental shortcuts based on social norms and stereotypes' (Guynn 2015). Biases can be based on skin colour, gender, age, height, weight, introversion versus extroversion, marital and parental status, disability status (for example, the use of a wheelchair or a cane), foreign accents, where someone went to college and more (Wilkie 2014).

This universal tendency towards unconscious bias exists because bias is rooted in the brain. Scientists have determined that it is found in the same region of the brain (the amygdala) associated with fear and threat. But bias is also found in other areas of the brain. Stereotyping, a form of bias, is associated with the temporal and frontal lobes. The left temporal lobe of the brain stores general information about people and objects and is the storage place for social stereotypes. The frontal cortex is associated with forming impressions of others, empathy and reasoning (Henneman 2014).

In other words, our brain evolved to mentally group things together to help make sense of the world. The brain categorizes all the information it is bombarded with and tags that information with general descriptions it can quickly sort information into. Bias occurs when those categories are tagged with labels like 'good' or 'bad' and are then applied to entire groups. Unconscious bias can also be caused by conditional learning. For example, if a person has a bad experience with someone they categorize as belonging to a particular group, they often associate that entire group with that bad experience (Venosa 2015).

From a survival point of view, this mental grouping into good or bad helped the brain make quick decisions about what was safe or not safe and what was appropriate or not appropriate. It was a developed survival mechanism hard-wired into our brains—and this makes it far more difficult to eliminate or minimize than originally thought (Ross 2008).

There is hope, however. One study found that hard-wired, unconscious brain bias can be reversed. The study found that between 2006 and 2013, the implicit preference (or unconscious bias) for straight people over gays and lesbians declined 13.4%. The author of the study acknowledged that while that percentage was significantly lower than the 26% decline in explicit preference (or expressed bias, if you will) during that same period, it showed that change can happen, albeit slowly, on an unconscious level (Jacobs 2015).

When we are unconsciously biased we may tend to think everything about a person is good because we like that person or we form stereotypes and assumptions about certain groups that mean it's impossible to make an objective judgement about members of those groups. We may also seek information that confirms pre-existing beliefs or assumptions.

Price (n.d.) introduced the concept of group think, a bias that occurs when people try too hard to fit into a group by mimicking others or holding back thoughts and opinions. This causes them to lose part of their identities and causes organizations to lose out on creativity and innovation.

How we conceive our students or their abilities will therefore have an unconscious impact on how we behave and treat them. Having an understanding and knowledge that such biases occur is useful as at least it makes us consciously aware of them.

What next?

'A journey of a thousand miles begins with a single step'
– Lao Tzu

When I started this journey and my research into mental health, resilience and well-being in HE, I really didn't expect to end with this book and the 'flourishing student model'. Writing this book has definitely been a journey of a thousand miles and every day, every week has meant taking a step towards something new. It has enabled me to 'test out' my own model (sometimes to the limit) and to see for myself how much any imbalances between my mental, physical, emotional, spiritual and social health have an impact on my own ability to flourish.

It certainly has taught me that I have a choice and that I am responsible for the outcomes I get in my life but most importantly that if I want to give my students advice, I also need to look after my own well-being and to make choices so that I can be an example to others and bring out the best in students and the belief that they cannot only enjoy but also flourish at university. Gandhi said that 'You must be the change you wish to see in the world.' This is what I am trying to achieve with this book and with what I do daily. My only hope is that reading this book will have the same effect on you. The conversations I had with students and with experts and colleagues have enabled me to create the model in this book and showed me that there are vital elements to flourishing.

Understanding

This means understanding what is going on in our lives, the differences between languishing and flourishing and between mental health and mental disorders (and what lies in between). But also understanding that our mental health is closely linked to our social, physical, emotional and spiritual health and that we need to look at ourselves and others holistically. Happiness is definitely an inside job but it isn't something permanent. There will always be challenging times and moments which are more difficult (ups and downs). Happiness is a journey not a destination. Mental health (and all the others) are a continuum and we cannot always be flourishing or always languishing; depending on the situations in our lives, we go up and down the scale.

Awareness

When we develop awareness, we become aware of our thoughts, emotions, feelings and sensations and we can accept and welcome them in our lives rather than fighting them or trying to control them. When we acknowledge what is happening in our life without judging it, we can then focus on finding a suitable solution.

A toolbox

Just like a plumber or an electrician has a toolbox for his or her work, it is extremely important for us to create and have our own toolbox of resources to help us in life. I'm hoping that you will be able to practise some of the exercises I introduce in the book and as a result keep them in your toolbox for resilience and well-being not just for yourself but also to share with other colleagues and with your tutees and students.

The flourishing student model was created based on the conversations I had with experts in the UK, Canada and the US, but most importantly by interviewing ten students based at various UK universities. The next step is to research further with more students to check the validity of this model with a larger group of participants and by investigating and analysing data sets. This is my project for next year.

From one colleague to another

Now that you have read this book and discovered this model, you may ask yourself how you can share your ideas or even get further training in Mindfulness.

I believe it's extremely useful to discuss and share experiences and challenges with other colleagues. It's both inspiring and motivating to discuss strategies and solutions with individuals from different institutions.

All the activities in this book have been shared with you to get you to test them out and to practise them on your own.

Sharing with others

Einstein stated that '*If you can't explain* it simply, *you don't understand* it well enough.' I believe that the more we share and discuss the ideas contained in this book, the better and easier it will be to apply and use them in our daily lives. Mindfulness is not simply a tool, it is a way of life. It is something that becomes engrained and habitual and that we do not think about but use naturally and regularly. This comes with time, patience and practice. We never get there… life is a journey and so there isn't a final destination.

If you would like to share your experience with others, feel free to join our Facebook page – The Flourishing Student.[25]

---

25 www.facebook.com/The-Flourishing-Student-1550247258566579/

This is a safe and supportive group where you can discuss the various methods, ask questions and share what worked well (or not so well) for you with other like-minded individuals.

For more information on workshops, events and training courses from the author of this book, check out www.flourishingstudent.com

Wishing you well on your journey to flourishing...

References

Abrams, M.P., Nicholas Carleton, R., Taylor, S. and Asmundson, G.J.G. 'Human tonic immobility: Measurement and correlates' in *Depression and Anxiety*, June, 26 (6), 550–556 (2009).

Abramson, L.Y., Seligman, M.E.P. and Teasdale, J. 'Learned helplessness in humans: Critique and reformulation' in *Journal of Abnormal Psychology*, 87, 49–74 (1978).

Adler, N.J. 'Re-entry: Managing cross-cultural transitions' in *Group & Organizational Studies*, 6, 341–356 (1981).

Adler, P.S. 'The transitional experience: An alternative view of culture shock' in *Journal of Humanistic Psychology*, 15 (4), 13–23 (1975).

Aiken, G.A. 'The potential effect of mindfulness meditation on the cultivation of empathy in psychotherapy: A qualitative inquiry' in *Dissertation Abstracts International, Section B: Sciences and Engineering*, 67, 2212 (2006).

American Psychiatric Association *Diagnostic and statistical manual of mental disorders* (5th ed.). Washington, DC. (2013).

Andrews, B. and Wilding, J.M. 'The relation of depression and anxiety to life-stress and achievement in students' in *British Journal of Psychology*, 95, 509–521 (2004).

Aschbacher, K., O'Donovan, A., Wolkowitz, O.M., Dhabhar, F.S., Su, Y. and Epel, E. 'Good stress, bad stress and oxidative stress: Insights from anticipatory cortisol reactivity' in *Psychoneuroendocrinology*, 38 (9), 1698–708 (2013).

Bandler, R. and Grinder, J. *The structure of magic I.* Paolo Alto, CA: Science and Behavior Books (1975).

Banks, S. *The missing link.* Vancouver, BC, Canada: Lone Pine (1998).

Baxter, A.J. 'Challenging the myth of an "epidemic" of common mental disorders: Trends in the global prevalence of anxiety and depression between 1990 and 2010' in *Depression and Anxiety,* 31, 506–516 (2014).

Beck, A.T. *Depression: Causes and treatment.* Philadelphia: University of Pennsylvania Press (1967).

Benard, B. *Fostering resiliency in kids: Protective factors in the family, school, and community.* Portland, OR: Western Center for Drug-Free Schools and Communities (1991).

Benard, B. *Resiliency: What we have learned.* Oakland, CA: WestEd (2004).

Bennett, T.H and Holloway, K.R. 'Drug misuse among university students in the UK: Implications for prevention' in *Substance Use & Misuse,* 49 (4), 448–455 (2013).

Bernstein, A. *The myth of stress: Where stress really comes from and how to live a happier and healthier life.* New York: Atria Books (2010).

Bewick, B.M., Gill, J. and Mulhern, B. 'Using electronic surveying to assess psychological distress within the UK university student population: A multi-site pilot investigation' in *E-Journal of Applied Psychology,* 4, 1–5 (2008).

Bierwisch, M. 'Some semantic universals of German adjectivals' in *Foundations of Language,* 3, 1–36 (1967).

Bohm, D. *Thought as a system.* Abingdon: Routledge (1994).

Boucher, J. and Osgood, C.E. 'The Pollyanna hypothesis' in *Journal of Verbal Learning and Verbal Behavior,* 8, 1–8 (1969).

Brabban, A. and Turkington, D. 'The search for meaning: Detecting congruence between life events, underlying schema and psychotic symptoms' in A.P. Morrison (ed.) *A casebook of cognitive therapy for psychosis,* 59–75. New York: Brunner-Routledge (2002).

Braden, G. *Fractal time: The secret of 2012 and a new world age.* New York, NY: Hay House (2012).

Cacioppo, J.T., Crites, S.L., Jr., Gardner, W.L. and Berntson, G.G. 'Bioelectrical echoes from evaluative categorizations: I. A late positive brain potential that varies as a function of trait negativity and extremity' in *Journal of Personality and Social Psychology,* 67, 115–125 (1994).

Cacioppo, J.T., Gardner, W.L. and Berntson, G.G. 'Beyond bipolar conceptualizations and measures: The case of attitudes and evaluative space' in *Personality and Social Psychology Review,* 1, 3–25 (1997).

Canfield, J. *The success principles: How to get from where you are to where you want to be.* New York: William Morrow Paperbacks; reprint edition (2006).

Cannon, W.B. *Bodily changes in pain, hunger, fear and rage, an account of recent researches into the function of emotional excitement.* New York and London: D. Appleton and Co. (1915).

Cannon, W.B. *Bodily changes in pain, hunger, fear, and rage* (2nd ed.). New York: Appleton-Century-Crofts (1929).

Cannon, W.B. *Wisdom of the body.* London: W.W. Norton & Company (1932).

Chambers, R., Gullone, E. and Allen, N.B. 'Mindful emotion regulation: An integrative review' in *Clinical Psychology Review,* 29, 560–572 (2009).

Chamorro-Premuzic, T. and Furnham, A. 'Personality predicts academic performance: Evidence from two longitudinal university samples' in *Journal of Research in Personality*, 37, 319–338 (2003a).

Chamorro-Premuzic, T. and Furnham, A. 'Personality traits and academic examination performance' in *European Journal of Personality*, 17, 237–250 (2003b).

Chomsky, N. *Current issues in linguistic theory*. The Hague: Mouton (1964).

Cicero, M.T. *Selected works*, translated by Michael Grant (2004).

Cline, F.W. and Fay, J. *Parenting with love and logic: Teaching children responsibility*. Colorado Springs, CO: Pinon Press (1990).

Cohn, P. 'How stress can affect sports performance' (2011). Available from www.peaksports.com/sports-psychology-blog/how-stress-can-affect-sports-performance/ [accessed 15/04/16].

Comer, R.J. *Abnormal psychology* (5th ed.). New York: Worth. Commission on Rehabilitation Counselor Certification (2004).

Corcoran, K.M., Farb, N., Anderson, A. and Segal, Z.V. 'Mindfulness and emotion regulation: Outcomes and possible mediating mechanisms' in A.M. Kring and D.M. Sloan (eds) *Emotion regulation and psychopathology: A transdiagnostic approach to etiology and treatment*. New York: Guilford Press, pp. 339-335 (2010).

Corrigan, P.W. 'Mental health stigma as social attribution: Implications for research methods and attitude change' in *Clinical Psychology: Science and Practice*, 7, 48–67 (2000).

Corrigan, P.W. 'How stigma interferes with mental health care' in *American Psychologist* (2004). Available from: citeseerx.ist.psu.edu/viewdoc/download?doi=10.1.1.379.4271&rep=rep1&type=pdf [accessed 11/09/16].

Coué, E. *Self mastery through conscious autosuggestion.* London (1922).

Coué, E. *How to practice suggestion and autosuggestion.* New York: American Library Service (1923).

Dalai Lama, and Cutler, Howard C. *The art of happiness: A handbook for living* (1999).

DeLaRosa, B. L., Spence, J.S., Shakal, S.K., Motes, M.A., Calley, C.S., Calley, V.I., Hart, J. Jr and Kraut, M.A. 'Electrophysiological spatiotemporal dynamics during implicit visual threat processing' in *Brain and Cognition*, 91, 54–61 (2014).

Dilts, R. *Changing belief systems with NLP.* London: Meta Publications (1990).

Dinan, T.G. and Cryan, J.F. 'The impact of gut microbiota on brain and behaviour: Implications for psychiatry' in *Current Opinions, Clinical Nutrition and Metabolic Care.* November;18 (6), 552–558 (2015).

Dunn, J.R. and Schweitzer, M.E. 'Feeling and believing: The influence of emotion on trust' in *Journal of Personality and Social Psychology*, 88, 736–748 (2005).

Dweck, C. *Mindset: The new psychology of success.* New York: Ballantine Books (2007).

Ecclestone, K. and Hayes, D. *The dangerous rise of therapeutic education.* London: Routledge (2009).

Egan, R., MacLeod, R., Jaye, C., McGee, R., Baxter, J. and Herbison, P. 'What is spirituality? Evidence from a New Zealand hospice study' in *Mortality*, 16 (4) (2011).

Emmons, R.A. and McCullough, M.E. 'Counting blessings versus burdens: An experimental investigation of gratitude and subjective well-being in daily life' in *Journal of Personality and Social Psychology*, 84, 377–389 (2003).

Farb, N.A.S., Segal, Z.C., Mayberg, H., Bean, J., McKeon, D., Fatima, Z. and Anderson, A.K. 'Attending to the present:

Mindfulness meditation reveals distinct neural modes of self-reference' in *Social Cognitive and Affective Neuroscience*, 2, 313–322 (2007).

Fardouly, J., Diedrichs, P.C., Vartanian, L. and Halliwell, E. 'Social comparisons on social media: The impact of Facebook on young women's body image concerns and mood' in *Body Image*, 13, 38–45 (2015).

Fromm, E. *The sane society*. Abingdon: Routledge Classics (2001).

Fromm-Reichmann, F. 'Loneliness' in *Psychiatry: Journal for the Study of Interpersonal Processes*, 22, 1–15 (1959).

Gottman, John M., Coan, James, Carrere, Sybil and Swanson, Catherine *Journal of Marriage and Family* Vol. 60, No. 1 (Feb., 1998), pp. 5-22: National Council on Family Relations DOI: 10.2307/353438 Stable URL: http://www.jstor.org/stable/353438

Gunaratana, H. *Mindfulness in plain English*. Somerville, MA: Wisdom Publications (2002).

Guynn, J. 'Google's "bias busting" workshops target hidden prejudices' in *USA Today* (12 May 2015). Available from: www.usatoday.com/story/tech/2015/05/12/google-unconsciousbias-diversity/27055485/ [accessed 06/09/16].

Haidt, J. *The Happiness hypothesis: Putting ancient wisdom and philosophy to the test of modern science*. Arrow Books: London (2006).

Henneman, T. *You, biased? No, it's your brain*. Workforce (2014). Available from: www.workforce.com/articles/20242-you-biased-no-its-your-brain. [accessed 06/09/16].

Hoffman, S.G., Sawyer, A.T., Witt, A.A. and Oh, D. 'The effect of mindfulness-based therapy on anxiety and depression: A metaanalytic review' in *Journal of Consulting and Clinical Psychology*, 78, 169–183 (2010).

Hughes, G. 'Transition distress: The big problem facing universities' in *Human Givens Journal*, 19, 42–44 (2012).

Hyman, Ira E. Jr.*, Benjamin, B, Sarb, A. and Wise-Swanson, Breanne M.'Failure to see money on a tree: Iattentional blindness for objects that guided behavior' in Frontiers in Psychology (23 April 2014) doi: 10.3389/fpsyg.2014.00356

Hyman, I. 'The dangers of going on autopilot' in *Psychology Today* (2014). Available from www.psychologytoday.com/blog/mental-mishaps/201404/the-dangers-going-autopilot [accessed 15/6/16].

Insel, Thomas (2013) https://www.nimh.nih.gov/about/directors/thomas-insel/blog/2013/transforming-diagnosis.shtml

Ivtzan, I., Hefferon, K. and Worth, P. *Second wave positive psychology: Embracing the dark side of life*. Abingdon: Routledge (2015).

Jacobs, T. 'Anti-gay bias is even diminishing on an unconscious level' in *Pacific Standard*. (2015) Available from: www.psmag.com/health-and-behavior/anti-gay-bias-is-evendiminishing-on-an-unconscious-level. [accessed 06/09/16].

Jacka, F.N., Kremer, P.J., Berk, M., de Silva-Sanigorski, A.M., Moodie, M. et al. 'A prospective study of diet quality and mental health in adolescents' in *PLoS ONE*, 6(9) (2011) Available from: e24805. doi:10.1371/journal.pone.0024805.

Jing-Schmidt, Z. 'Negativity bias in language: A cognitive affective model of emotive intensifiers' in Cognitive Linguistics, 18, 417-433 (2007) Available from: 10.1515/COG.2007.023. Joseph, J. *The resilient child*. New York, NY: Insight Books (1994).

Kabat-Zinn, J. *Wherever you go, there you are: Mindfulness meditation in everyday life*. New York: Hyperion (1994).

Kadam, S. and Kotate, P.A 'Theoretical perspective of the effects of assumptions on emotional well-being of an individual' in *International Journal of Indian Psychology*, 3 (4), No 75 (2016).

Keller, A., Litzelman, K., Eisk, L.E., Maddox, T., Cheung, E.R., Creswell, P.D., et al. 'Does the perception that stress affects health matter? The association with health and mortality' in *Health Psychology*, 31, 677–681 (2012).

Keyes, C.L.M. 'The mental health continuum: From languishing to flourishing in life' in *Journal of Health and Social Behavior*, 43, 207–222 (2002).

Keyes, C.L.M. 'Complete mental health: An agenda for the 21st century' in C.L.M. Keyes and J. Haidt (eds), *Flourishing: Positive psychology and the life well-lived*, Washington, DC: American Psychological Association, 293–312 (2003).

Kihlstrom, J.F., Mulvaney, S., Tobias, B.A. and Tobis, I.P. 'The emotional unconscious' in E. Eich, J.F. Kihlstrom, G.H. Bower, J.P. Forgas and P.M. Niedenthal (eds), *Cognition and emotion* (30–86) New York: Oxford University Press (2000).

Killingsworth, M.A. and Gilbert, D.T. 'A wandering mind is an unhappy mind' in *Science*, November 12; 330 (6006), 932 (2010).

Kingdon, D.G. and Turkington, D. 'The use of cognitive behavior therapy with a normalizing rationale in schizophrenia. Preliminary report' in *Journal of Nervous and Mental Disease*, 179(4), 207–211 (1991).

Kingsbury, E. 'The relationship between empathy and mindfulness: Understanding the role of self-compassion' in *Dissertation Abstracts International: Section B: Science and Engineering*, 70 (3175) (2009).

Korzybski, A. *Science and sanity: An introduction to non-Aristotelian systems and general semantics.* Fort Worth, TX: Institute of General Semantics; 5th edition (1933/1995)

Kreitz, C., Furley, P., Memmert, D. and Simons, D.J. 'Inattentional blindness and individual differences in cognitive abilities' in *PLoS ONE*, 10 (8), e0134675 (2015).

Kutcher, S.P., Wei, Y. and Weist, M.D. *School mental health: Global challenges and opportunities.* Cambridge: Cambridge University Press (2015).

Lao, T. *Lao-Tzu's Taoteching,* translated by Porter, Bill (Red Pine) (3rd Revised ed.), Port Townsend, WA: Copper Canyon Press (2009).

LeDoux, J. *The emotional brain.* London: Orion Books (1998).

Leitch, L. 'The nervous system and resilience' Threshold Global-Works (2015). Available from: *www.thresholdglobalworks.com/pdfs/nervous-system-and-resilience.pdf. [Accessed 11/09/16].*

Lifton, R.J. *The protean self: Human resilience in an age of transformation.* New York: Basic Books (1993).

Locke, J., Campbell, M.A. and Kavanagh, D.J. 'Can a parent do too much for their child? An examination by parenting professionals of the concept of overparenting' in *Australian Journal of Guidance and Counselling,* 22(2), pp. 249–265 (2012).

Loehr, J. and Schwartz, T. *The power of full engagement: Managing energy, not time, is the key to high performance and personal renewal.* New York: Free Press (2005).

Macmin, L. and Foskett, J. '"Don't be afraid to tell." The spiritual and religious experience of mental health service users in Somerset' in *Mental Health, Religion & Culture,* 7 (1), 23–40 (2004).

Mandler, G. 'Presidential address to Division 1 (General Psychology) of the American Psychological Association. Consciousness: Its function and construction' Centre for Human Information Processing. University of California at San Diego, June 1983.

Mayberg, H.S., Lozano, A.M., Voon, V., McNeely, H.E., Seminowicz, D. 'Deep brain stimulation for treatment-resistant depression' in *Neuron*, 45 (5), 651–660 (2005).

McCrae, R.R. and Costa, P.T. 'Validation of the five factor model of personality across instruments and observers' in *Journal of Personality and Social Psychology*, 52(1), 81–90 (1987).

McGowan, P.O., Sasaki, A., D'Alessio, A.C., Dymov, S., Labonté, B. 'Epigenetic regulation of the glucocorticoid receptor in human brain associates with childhood abuse' in *Nature Neuroscience*, 12, 342–348 (2009).

McMartin, S.E., Kingsbury, M., Dykxhoorn, J. and Colman, I. 'Time trends in symptoms of mental illness in children and adolescents in Canada' in *CMAJ: Canadian Medical Association Journal*, 186(18), E672–E678 (2014).

McNally, R.J. *What is mental illness?* Cambridge, MA: Belknap Press (2011).

McWilliams, P. *Do it! Let's get off our buts.* Nashville, TN: Prelude Press (1994).

Merton, T. *Thoughts in solitude.* New York: Farrar, Straus and Giroux (2011).

Monroe, S.M. and Hadjiyannakis, H. 'The social environment and depression: Focusing on severe life stress' in I.H. Gotlib and C.L. Hammen (eds), *Handbook of depression* (314–340). New York: Guilford Press (2002).

Moore, A. and Malinowski, P. 'Meditation, mindfulness and cognitive flexibility' in *Consciousness and Cognition*, 18, 176–186 (2009).

Munich, R.L. and Munich, M.A. 'Overparenting and the narcissistic pursuit of attachment' in Psychiatric *Annals*, 39, 227–235 (2009).

Neff, L.A. and Karney, B.R. 'Stress and reactivity to daily relationship experiences: How stress hinders adaptive processes in marriage' in *Journal of Personality and Social Psychology*, 97 (3), 435–450 (2009).

Newsome, S., Christopher, J.C., Dahlen, P. and Christopher, S. 'Teaching counselors self-care through mindfulness practices' in *Teachers College Record*, 108, 1881–1990 (2006).

Nietzsche, F. *Twilight of the idols* (R. Polt, trans.) Indianapolis, IN: Hackett (1997/1889).

Oberg, K. 'Culture shock: Adjustment to new cultural environments' in *Practical Anthropology*, 7, 177–182 (1960).

Ortner, C.N.M., Kilner, S.J. and Zelazo, P.D. 'Mindfulness meditation and reduced emotional interference on a cognitive task' in *Motivation and Emotion*, 31, 271–283 (2007).

Orwell, G. 'Politics and the English language' in *Horizon*, April (1946).

Pen, D.L. and Martin, J. 'The stigma of severe mental illness: Some potential solutions for a recalcitrant problem' in *Psychiatric Quarterly*, 69 (3), 235–247 (1998).

Peplau, L.A. and Perlman, D. 'Perspectives on loneliness' in L.A. Peplau and D. Perlman (eds), *Loneliness: A sourcebook of current theory, research and therapy* (1–18). New York: Wiley (1982).

Pert, C. *Molecules of emotion: The science behind mind-body medicine.* New York: First Touchstone Edition (1999).

Pollan, M. 'The intelligent plan' *New Yorker*, 23 December. (2013). Available from: www.newyorker.com/magazine/2013/12/23/the-intelligent-plant [accessed 11/12/16].

Price, S. 'Think slow' BCCJacumen.com. (n.d.). Available from: www.priceglobal.com/media/documents/603778102_BCCJ%20UCB-SP.pdf [accessed 11/09/16].

Richardson, A., King, S., Garrett, R. and Wrench, A. 'Thriving or just surviving? Exploring student strategies for a smoother transition to university. A practice report' in *The International Journal of the First Year in Higher Education*, 3 (2), 87–93 (2012).

Rideout, V.J., Foher, U.G. and Roberts, D.F. 'Generation M2: Media in the lives of 8–18-year-Olds: A Kaiser Family Foundation study. Menlo Park, California' (2010). Available from: kaiserfamilyfoundation.files.wordpress.com/2013/01/8010.pdf (PDF, 2.73MB). [accessed 12/01/17].

Roberts, R., Golding, J., Towell, T., Reid, S., Woodford, S., Vetere, A. and Weinreb, I. 'Mental and physical health in students: The role of economic circumstances' in *British Journal of Health Psychology*, 5(3), 289–297 (2000).

Rogers, C. *On becoming a person: A therapists' view of psychotherapy*. New York: Mariner Books; 2nd ed. (1995).

Rosenhan, D. 'On being sane in insane places' in *Science*, 179 (4070), 250–258. doi:10.1126/science.179.4070.250. PMID 4683124. Archived from the original on 17 November 2004 (1973).

Rosenthal, R. and Jacobson, L. 'Pygmalion in the classroom' in *The Urban Review* 3 (16), 16–20 (1968).

Ross, H. 'Exploring unconscious bias. Diversity best practices' (2008). Available from: www.cookross.com/docs/UnconsciousBias.pdf [accessed 11/09/16].

Royal College of Psychiatrists. 'Mental health of students in Higher Education (CR166)' (2011). Available from: www.rcpsych.ac.uk/publications/collegereports/cr/cr166.aspx [accessed 16/08/17].

Rozin, P. and Royzman, E.B. 'Negativity bias, negativity dominance, and contagion' in *Personality and Social Psychology Review*, 5 (4), 296–320 (2001).

Russell, T.A. and Siegmund, G. 'What and who? Mindfulness in the mental health setting' in *BJPsych Bulletin*, 40 (6), 333–340 (2016).

Sawyer, R.K. 'Optimizing learning: Implications of learning sciences research' in OECD/CERI, *Focus in Learning: Searching for Alternatives*. Paris: OECD/CERI (2007).

Sax, L.J. 'Health trends among college freshmen' in *Journal of American College Health*, 45, 252–262 (1997).

Schneiderman, N., Ironson, G. and Siegel, S.D. 'Stress and health: Psychological, behavioral, and biological determinants' in *Annual Review of Clinical Psychology*, 1, 607–628 (2005).

Schure, M.B., Christopher, J. and Christopher, S. 'Mind-body medicine and the art of self care: Teaching mindfulness to counseling students through yoga, meditation and qigong' in *Journal of Counseling and Development*, 86, 47–56 (2008).

Segrin, C., Woszidlo, A., Givertz, M., Bauer, A. and Taylor Murphy, M. 'The association between overparenting, parent-child communication, and entitlement and adaptive traits in adult children' in *Family Relations*, 61, 237–252 (2012).

Senge, P.M. *The fifth discipline: The art & practice of the learning organization*. New York: Doubleday/Currency (1990).

Shakespeare, W., in Thompson, A. and Taylor, N. (eds) *Hamlet: The texts of 1603 and 1623*. London: The Arden Shakespeare (2006).

Shapiro, S.L. and Carlson, L.E. *The art and science of mindfulness: Integrating mindfulness into psychology and the helping professions*. Washington, DC: American Psychological Association (2009).

Shaw, A., Joseph, S. and Linley, P.A. 'Religion, spirituality, and posttraumatic growth: A systematic review' in *Mental Health, Religion & Culture*, 8 (1) (2005).

Siegel, D.J. 'Mindfulness training and neural integration: Differentiation of distinct streams of awareness and the cultivation of wellbeing' in *Social Cognitive and Affective Neuroscience*, 2, 259–263 (2007a).

Siegel, D.J. *The mindful brain: Reflection and attunement in the cultivation of well-being.* New York: Norton (2007b).

Tang, Y., Ma, Y., Wang, J., Fan, Y., Feng, S., Lu, Q. and Posner, M.I. 'Short-term meditation training improves attention and self-regulation' in *PNAS* Proceedings of the National Academy of Sciences of the United States of America, 104, 17152–17156 (2007).

Teitelbaum, J. *Real cause, real cure.* Emmaus, PA: Rodale Books (2012).

Universities UK. 'Higher education in numbers' (n.d.). Available from: www.universitiesuk.ac.uk/facts-and-stats/Pages/higher-education-data.aspx [accessed 15/8/16].

US Office of the Surgeon General; Center for Mental Health Services; National Institute of Mental Health 'Mental health: Culture, race, and ethnicity: A supplement to mental health: A report of the Surgeon General'. Rockville (MD): Substance Abuse and Mental Health Services Administration (US) Publications and Reports of the Surgeon General (2001).

Venosa, A. 'Prejudice in the brain—How evolutionarily valuable brain processes have turned problematic' in *Medical Daily* (2015). Available from: www.medicaldaily.com/prejudice-brain-how-evolutionarily-valuable-brain-processeshave-turned-problematic-344368 [accessed 11/09/16].

Walsh, R. and Shapiro, S.L. 'The meeting of meditative disciplines and western psychology: A mutually enriching dialogue' in *American Psychologist*, 61, 227–239 (2006).

Wang, S.J. 'Mindfulness meditation: Its personal and professional impact on psychotherapists' in *Dissertation Abstracts*

International: Section B: Science and Engineering, 67, 4122 (2007).

Warburton, D.E.R., Nicol, C.W. and Bredin, S.S.D. 'Health benefits of physical activity: The evidence' in *CMAJ: Canadian Medical Association Journal,* 174 (6), 801–809 (2006).

Waugh, C.E., Wager, T.D., Fredrickson, B.L., Noll, D.C. and Taylor, S.F. 'The neural correlates of trait resilience when anticipating and recovering from threat' in *Social Cognitive and Affective Neuroscience,* 3, 322–332 (2008).

Weaver, I.C.G., Cervoni, N., Champagne, F.A., D'Alessio, A.C., Sharma, S., Seckl, J.R., Dymov, S., Szyf, M. and Meaney, M.J. 'Epigenetic programming by maternal behaviour' in *Nature Neuroscience,* 7, 847–854 (2004).

Weir, K. 'The roots of mental illness. How much of mental illness can the biology of the brain explain?' *Monitor on Psychology,* 43 (6), 32 Washington DC: American Psychological Association (2012).

Werner, E.E. and Smith R.S. *Overcoming the odds: High risk children from birth to adulthood.* Ithaca, NY: Cornell University Press (1992).

Wilkie, D. 'Rooting out hidden bias' in *SHRM* (2014) Available from: www.shrm.org/publications/hrmagazine/editorialcontent/2014/1214/pages/1214-hidden-bias.aspx [accessed 11/09/16].

Williams, J.M.G. 'Mindfulness and psychological process' in *Emotion,* 10, 1–7 (2010).

Winch, G. 'Why we all need to practice emotional first aid' November (2014) TEDx Linnaeus University. Available from: www.ted.com/talks/guy_winch_the_case_for_emotional_hygiene/footnotes [accessed 06/01/17].

Wood, D.J., Bruner, J.S. and Ross, G. 'The role of tutoring in problem solving' in *Journal of Child Psychiatry and Psychology,* 17 (2), 89–100 (1976).

Wooden, J. *A lifetime of observations and reflections on and off the court* London: McGraw-Hill Education (1997).

World Health Organization (WHO) 'The ICD-10 classification of mental and behavioural disorders—diagnostic criteria for research'. Geneva: World Health Organization (1993).

World Health Organization (WHO) 'Skills for health. Skills-based health education including life skills: An important component of a child-friendly/health-promoting school' (2003) Available from: www.who.int/school_youth_health/media/en/sch_skills4health_03.pdf [accessed 16/5/16].

World Health Organization (WHO) 'Promoting mental health: Concepts, emerging evidence, practice (Summary Report)'. Geneva: World Health Organization (2004).

World Health Organization (WHO) 'Promoting mental health: Concepts, emerging evidence, practice'. Geneva: World Health Organization (2005).

World Health Organization (WHO) ICD-11 beta draft (2014). Available from: apps.who.int/classifications/icd11/browse/l-m/en (accessed 21/01/16).

Yeager, D.S., Johnson, R., Spitzer, B.J., Trzesniewski, K.H., Powers, J. and Dweck, C.S. 'The far-reaching effects of believing people can change: Implicit theories of personality shape stress, health, and achievement during adolescence' in *Journal of Personality and Social Psychology*, 106 (6), 867–884 (2014).

Zubin, J. and Spring, B. 'Vulnerability: A new view of schizophrenia' in *Journal of Abnormal Psychology*, 86, 103–126 (1977).

Index